# THE AMERICAN WAY OF LIFE

# The American
# Way of Life

## ALI A. SHUKAIR
*Fort Valley State College*

PHILOSOPHICAL LIBRARY
New York

*"man" is that being who is not
what he ought to be.*

# Table of Contents

*Preface* ...................................... ix

*Introduction* ................................ xi

I. DREAM AND REALITY ......................... 1

II. THE AMERICAN POTENTIAL .................... 9

III. SOCIALIZATION OF THE INDIVIDUAL .............. 16

IV. RELIGION: COMMITMENT AND COMPROMISE ...... 25

V. DISCRIMINATION IN THE UNITED STATES .......... 43

VI. ADVERTISING IN AMERICA ..................... 68

VII. MASS COMMUNICATION: HOW IT AFFECTS
AMERICAN SOCIETY ......................... 82

VIII. THE AMERICANS' LACK OF KNOWLEDGE OF
OTHER COUNTRIES ......................... 90

IX. FREEDOM AND ALIENATION IN AMERICAN SOCIETY.. 97

X. THE SEXUAL REVOLUTION WITHIN THE AMERICAN
SOCIETY: INDIVIDUAL RELATIONSHIP TO FAMILY
AND COMMUNITY .......................... 105

XI. PEOPLE IN THE UNITED STATES AND HOW THEY
USE THEIR LEISURE TIME ................... 117

*Bibliography* ................................ 124

# Preface

No one knows me better than I know myself, and no one knows how inadequate the judge is better than the judge himself; but the struggle shall remain. . . . A struggle between contradictions. All shall judge, and all shall be judged. . . . Each time the judgment will be inadequate because of the "I" saying, "Thou shalt not judge."

In order to provide the judges with less room for inadequate judgment, it is better that the subject expose himself completely. The greater and more complete the exposition, the more adequate the judgment, provided the judges are not prejudiced and provided the subject is original, sincere and true to the experience. To this creed I am committed, and it is my belief that the sooner we start teaching for this state of affairs the sooner we will realize the creativity necessary for real human survival and elevation. Unfortunately, I hold the belief of the small minority; the minority that upholds the right to dissent when the majority compromise.

Whatever the judgment may be, what I have to say here is mine, and I am fully responsible for it. I do not apologize for those who might feel offended by it; on the contrary, I will advise them to refute it if they can justly do so. For this is the best possible means of arriving at the right social choice.

ALI SHUKAIR

# Introduction

This work is the result of almost twenty years spent in the United States: five years (1952-1957) as a foreign student in the United States; five years (1957-1962) as a permanent resident of the United States; more than nine years (1962- ) as an American citizen. The first twenty years of my life were spent in Jordan, so this work may be considered as that of an "outsider" to the American culture.

I have tried to view American life with anthropological detachment, as far as that is possible for one who lived it for nineteen years. That is to say, I have tried to keep a certain emotional distance from the subject; though, at times, this emotional distance is hard to maintain.

One part of this work deals with how America is viewed from the outside, and how it is viewed from the inside. What kind of ideas one has of America before coming to it, and what one finds America to be after being in it. I chose the title for this part to be "Dream and Reality."

The other parts of this work deal with the different aspects of American life that I found incompatible with American ideals, as well as with some aspects of life that are compatible with the ideals but with a great gap between the two. A major part of this work is dedicated to education and the function of education in American life as well as life in general.

My sources for what is stated are primarily my personal experiences and observations. Other sources are different books written on the subject, as well as articles that appeared in literary and professional periodicals and newspapers.

This work as a whole is intended as a *constructive* criticism of American life. Though I hold the view that American life is one of the best in existence, I do believe that there is room for improving it.

# THE AMERICAN WAY OF LIFE

THE AMERICAN WAY OF DEATH

# CHAPTER I

# Dream and Reality

The first part of this chapter deals with the kind of ideas I had of America and the American people while I was in Jordan. Some of these ideas were conveyed to me by some of my Jordanian acquaintances who had visited the United States and returned to Jordan. What they had to say about the United States was reinforced by Hollywood movies shown in my part of the world. Most of the ideas I held of the States, however, were due to my attending an American high school in Ramallah, Jordan for three years; namely, the Friends Boys School.

One of the ideas I held of the United States, while in Jordan, is that America is "one nation under God, indivisible, with liberty and justice for *all*." It is a "great family of free men and women." And, among the many blessings in America is the solemn responsibility, "the duty to help maintain and advance the principles and ideals upon which our Republic was founded and built." [1]

Another of the ideas I held is that among the qualities of a good American are the following five:

1. The good American cherishes democratic values and bases his actions on them. He has respect for the dignity and worth of human personality. He is concerned with the general welfare of all people; he believes that human culture belongs to all men. He is loyal to equality of opportunity for all. "All other characteristics of the good citizen stem from, and are part of, this primary quality."

[1] "Welcome to U.S.A. Citizenship," United States Department of Justice, M-76.

1

2. The good citizen practices democratic human relationships in the family, school, community, and the larger scenes. He recognizes the interdependence of all people in all scenes. He sincerely desires to help other persons.

3. The good citizen recognizes the social problems of the times and has the will and the ability to work toward their solution. He endeavors to help in the solution of problems of race, religion, economics, and politics; problems of the United States in world affairs; problems of the equitable use of resources; and problems of family, school, community and neighborhood living.

4. The good citizen is aware of and takes responsibility for meeting basic human needs. He is aware of the importance of meeting human needs and is concerned with the extension of the essentials of life to more individuals. All people have certain basic human needs; the need to be free from aggression, domination, or exploitation; the need for love and affection; the need to belong to groups and to be helped by others; the need to take responsibility in cooperation with others; the need for a level of living which provides for adequate health, housing, and recreation; the need to have high standards of spiritual, ethical, and moral values. The failure to meet these fundamental human needs may result in the development of maladjustments which increase the intensity of social problems.

5. The good citizen possesses and uses knowledge, skills, and abilities necessary in the democratic society. These are gained through facility in reading, listening, discussing, and observing. He uses these skills and abilities to gain understanding of the present structure and functioning of society, and the working principles of representative government, the impact of pressure groups, the operation of the economic system, the social stratification of the population, and the relation of all these to the complex social heritage. With these possessions, the good citizen becomes more proficient in civic action.[2]

All these, among others, are qualities of a good citizen;

[2] "Detroit Citizenship Education Study," as quoted in *A Curriculum for Citizenship*, Arnold R. Meier, et al., (Detroit: Wayne University Press, 1952), pp. 15-16.

and this is the type of American citizen known to me before coming to the United States. In short, the idea conveyed to me before coming to the United States was that the Americans have and do enjoy everything, and that America is "Heaven" on earth.

This was the dream, and it lasted until I got to Southern Illinois University during September, 1952. Though I woke up to that dream sometime after 1952, I find the dream still present in my mind, and I keep on working to turn it into reality.

After being in the United States long enough to see more of it, and more of the American people and their ways, what I had been led to believe before coming to the States did seem to me as a dream. My being in the United States made me think as though I had been in a beautiful dream and, waking up, found that things in the States are simply not what I have "seen" them to be in the dream.

I found Americans to be human. They are just as human as Arabs, British, French, and Jews, but not more so. In fact, I found many of them to be less human in certain cases, especially in their treatment of Negroes, American Indians, and certain other minority groups. I was shocked to find out that there are even separate churches for whites and Negroes of the same denomination, let alone other areas of discrimination. Looking deeper into this phenomenon, I later found that there is an "Other America" [3] which is seldom heard or seen.

Leaving prejudice and certain sentiments aside, most Americans are kind and innocent. When asked, they usually help even if they have to go out of their way to do it at times. Though this might not be true of people in large towns, it seems to be prevalent in middle-sized towns and small towns. There is a general sociability and ease of intercourse among Americans, that I doubt exists among other civilized people. This general sociability and ease of intercourse is facilitated by the average American's concern and keeping up with the seasonal sports. Sports provide Americans with a common de-

[3] Harrington, Michael, *The Other America.*

3

nominator necessary for intercourse. "Who won today?" is one of the most puzzling questions I was asked when I first came to America. To an American this question is one of the best ways to start a conversation, and needless to say, it is a question that most American males could answer without hesitation. "What is new?" or "What do you know?" are other questions that are often heard.

I found most Americans to be highly ignorant of other countries, peoples, customs, history, and aspirations. On the whole, the American people are isolationists. They are mostly engrossed in their personal problems and interests.

I found most Americans to be in a "hurry." Most of them are always rushing, only to get nowhere. This is simply because they have no time. Time is one of the few things not found in America. Americans are in a mad rush and seldom have time to explore things in depth, unless there is "something in it for them." "What is in it for me?" is the question whose answer determines whether the American will explore the issue or not. As such, they seldom know enough about their own history and geography, let alone the history and geography of other countries. The sources of information available to the American are the same ones available to people in other countries. These sources are the schools, the movies, the communication media, and foreign travel. These sources are very deficient and inadequate. Sometimes they are even unreliable. The school is certainly deficient in the area of information about other countries, both in curriculum and in teacher preparation. The press is not only deficient but also gives mis-information at times. Even if the press did give the right information about other countries, the average reader would not read it.

I also found most Americans operating on the business ethic. That is to say, one must have in order to get more of what he has; or as the old saying goes, one must have money in order to make money. This ethic, I found, permeates most aspects of life in America. If one is in the market to borrow money, he must have "credit," otherwise he is likely not to get it; if one is not already indebted, or has no credit, he might not be able to borrow. Of course, if one has money, he can

4

easily borrow more; why? Any sensible businessman will then come to his "rescue" and loan him the amount he needs. Also, if one respects others, the others usually will not respect him; if he does not respect them, they usually would respect him. That is, if one needs others, others do not satisfy his need; if he does not need them, then they will need him.

I found America to be the land of advertisement. Almost everything is advertised in America, from going to church to going to sleep. Even some advertisements are themselves advertised. This business of advertising raises a fundamental moral issue. I am here alluding to the use of psychologists in the manipulation of the individual's mind and making up his mind for him. That is to say, make him a victim of the advertisement through the use of the right words in order to entice him.

I found Americans to be highly tolerant of other nationality groups. Due to the social mobility and intermarriage among the different nationalities, the "family tree" of the average American includes more than two nationalities. This makes for the ready acceptance of other nationality groups. If they could utilize this process and extend it to include "color" and/ or race problems, they would do much to solve these two problems.

I found most Americans to possess a certain commonness of mind, and I also found them to be insensible to the nobler aspects of life. They all seem to "think" alike. The Americans may be divided into three groups. There are "little" people who spend the time talking about other people; there are "big" people who spend the time talking about things; and there are very few people comprising the third group. These are the "thinking" people, who spend the time talking about ideas. The majority of the Americans according to this division are "big" people.

I found most Americans to be quite realistic, especially in realtion to others. They accept most things as these things happen to be at the time. As such, they don't strive to change things. What I mean to say here is that to most Americans, "to be realistic" means to accept whatever happens unless the happening affects the interests of the majority, directly and negatively. This becomes very evident when a certain situation is discussed with them. If the situation does not directly and negatively affect them, they would usually, after the discussion, say, "Yes, that situation might be unjust; *but* that is the way it is, and it is futile to try to do anything about it." In other words, it is irrelevant whether something is just or unjust unless "it hits close to home."

I found most Americans to be highly regimented. This regimentation is the result of many factors, I am sure; but the most important of these factors is mass communication. Collective action is very important for the progress of civilization. Collective action on the part of Americans seem to be nothing more than the age-old idea of "security in numbers." This idea is reinforced in American society by the overwhelming use of statistics. Because of this "security in numbers" idea, most Americans are submissive, subservient, and conforming. Independence, individuality, and dissent, which are the main characteristics of a democracy, are no longer qualities of the average American. These qualities are found only in a very small number of Americans who are usually looked upon with suspicion by the average American. The right to dissent is almost non-existent except for an extremely small number of intellectuals.

I found most Americans possessing most of the material comforts available to man at present. America is, no doubt, the most prosperous country in the world. Most Americans are constantly thinking of a "higher standard of living." The standard of living index seems to be a very important substitute of morality in America.

Along with all this prosperity, I found most Americans to be anxious and insecure. Among the many factors that lead to anxiety and insecurity is man's capability to destroy the whole civilization. This ability to destroy is more real to those who possess the weapons. As such, it is real to the Americans. The presence of Russia with its capability of destruction, America's enmity to Russia, and the eventual possibility of a confrontation in terms of atomic bombs and nuclear missiles increase the anxiety and the insecurity in the people. The competitive at-

6

mosphere and the alienation of the individual through this competition in the United States is another important factor.

In spite of the competitive struggle and the alienation that the average American is subjected to, he is very generous with the money he earns. While most Americans do prize the money they get, as an indication of their ability, and consequently as proof of their worthiness, and as such, prefer to earn the money they get, they are readily generous with it. It might be that this generosity is a cover-up for the insecurity and the anxiety they experience.

I found most Americans to be honest, smiling, and ambiguous. They are so honest that they would believe almost anything they hear. Oaths, which are considered by many as the last resort of liars, are required only in areas where lying is expected. Thus, in the courts one is supposed to take an oath. And, because of the average American's mistrust for those who serve the public, public servants are also required to take a "loyalty" oath. This is certainly a poor way to find out whether or not an individual is honest or loyal. The oath is seldom a good guide to future good conduct.

On the average, the American is characterized by what might look like a warm, inviting smile. Though this smile is not as common today as it used to be in the nineteen fifties, it is still prevalent. It is an artificial, funny smile rather than a genuine one. In most cases, this smile is meaningless, but it does add to the ambiguity that is also characteristic of Americans. Though ambiguity is a characteristic of politicians everywhere, in America it is not restricted to them. The average American seldom tells in plain language what he intends to do or what he means to say. He does not like to commit himself to a specific point of view, for that would render him incapable of shifting course without being accused of inconsistency. As such, he would remain ambiguous in so far as he can.

I found most Americans to be spectators and compromisers. Because of their ambiguous positions, they are able to compromise without much "loss of face." Their ability to compromise is one of the main factors that makes them spectators. Laxity in moral standards, where the only moral standard left

7

is that of negating all moral standards, is another factor leading to compromise and spectation.

Americans love to watch things. If they are not watching television at home, they would be at a sports event, at the movies, or at some other form of passive entertainment. They have much free time, but they have not learned how to turn it into leisure or meaningful activities. Free time to them means "unoccupied" time which one can spend as one pleases, preferably with no effort on the part of the individual.

# CHAPTER II

# The American Potential

"We alone do good to our neighbors not upon a calculation of interest, but in the confidence of freedom and in a frank and fearless spirit." [1] This is one of the reasons Pericles gave for his proclamation in his funeral oration that Athens was the school of Hellas; that is, because only Athens obeyed the dictates of highest morality. During the Peloponnesian War, however, this ideal was transformed into a mere struggle for power, where morality is traded for expediency. This remains as the main problem today. This age-old conflict between ideal principles and sheer power in the service of self-interest still survives. It is as present in the United States as it was in Athens, and, I am afraid, as it will remain for a long time to come. President Eisenhower recognized this in his farewell television address on January 17, 1961.

> Our military organization today bears little relation to that known of any of my predecessors in peacetime—or, indeed, by the fighting men of World War II or Korea.
> Until the latest of our world conflicts, the United States had no armaments industry, American makers of plow-shares could, with time and as required, make swords as well.
> But we can no longer risk emergency improvisation of national defense. We have been compelled to create a

---

[1] *The History of Thucydides,* trans. by Benjamin Jowett (New York: The Tandy-Thomas Company, 1909), Book ii, 40, p. 199.

permanent armaments industry of vast proportions. Added to this, three and a half million men and women are directly engaged in the defense establishment. We annually spend on military security alone more than the net income of all United States corporations.

Now this conjunction of an immense military establishment and a large arms industry is new in the American experience. The total influence—economic, political, even spiritual—is felt in every city, every state house, every office of the Federal Government. We recognize the imperative need for this development. Yet we must not fail to comprehend its grave implications. Our toil, resources and livelihood are all involved; so is the very structure of our society.

In the councils of government, we must guard against the acquisition of unwarranted influence, whether sought or unsought, by the military-industrial complex. The potential for the disastrous rise of misplaced power exists and will persist. . . .

Among other things, "The United States made two outstanding contributions: one, it contributed greatly to the advance of technology, and two, it established a regime of political liberty over a vast region." [2] These words, according to a conversation with George S. Counts, are the words of the great American historian Charles A. Beard in answer to a Chinese educator. Indeed, the great technological and political revolutions that have found a comfortable home in the United States are two of the greatest factors that led to the shattering and passing away of traditional society and rigid social orders, and to the final emancipation of man in the form of individual freedom and free association.

The flowering of science and technology gave man an enormous power to explore nature and control it so as to provide himself with the conveniences necessary to transform his life. The industrial society, created by science and technology, is the most successful way of life mankind has ever known. This

---

[2] George Sylvester Counts, the American educator and distinguished professor, is my advisor in this work.

is reflected by the abundance in almost every aspect of life. Due to this technology and industrialization people eat better, sleep better, have more comfortable dwellings, travel more and in more comfort, and live faster, longer, and more meaningful lives than ever before. The scientific-industrial revolution, through which all the above became available, should, if man chooses so, bring about a fuller realization of his highest ideals.

It is reasonable to say that freedom is, to a very large degree, dependent on the further development of science and technology. Because of this development in the United States, the United States is the only country that is able to transform its society through just and peaceful means, without bloody revolutions.

> . . . We (Americans) have firmer ground for hope than any previous generation has ever had, precisely because of the technological threshold on which we now clearly see that we are standing. Men have always sought security, or, as Dewey called it, certainty. They have always dreamed of better things; and if they could see no hope of better things in this world—for themselves, but even more for their children and their children's children —they have dreamed of other worlds beyond pearl-studded gates, where the streets would be paved with gold, and milk and honey would flow in the gutters. It is only since the effects of the great technological revolution of modern times began to be apparent that boldly imaginative men began to catch sight of the possibility of general abundance here and now. . . .
>
> And what is true of abundance is true of all real values, which indeed are indissociable from abundance as they are indissociable from each other. Freedom is a necessary condition to the attainment of abundance, and abundance is a necessary condition to the attainment of freedom. Freedom is possible only among equals, and equality is possible only when men are free from arbitrary social distinctions. These values are attainable only when men have achieved a measure of security; and real security is possible only when men have achieved a measure of

abundance and a reasonable prospect of its continuance. But it is also possible only for those who enjoy freedom among equals; for any other condition implies a threat to security. And the same is true of the highest achievements of the human spirit. . . .

Such is the industrial way of life. It is a way of life to which modern man has dedicated himself because it is the epitome of the real values which take their meaning from the life process of mankind. And its supreme value is hope—a hope, warranted by past achievements—of a far better life next year for ourselves, in the next century for our children's children, and in the next millennium for all mankind.[3]

Industrialism created big cities where man *may* exercise his need to socialize at a large scale. The advance in science and technology created mass communication where man *may* exercise his need to commune with a great number of selves. The knowledge and know-how available have created an atmosphere where man *may* exercise his need to be free and not dictated to by an outside agent. This last one is man's need to think and express himself freely, without hindrance from traditional religion, parents, family, or nation. The Americans, today, seem to be freed from all of these with the exception of the nation. The nation still dictates, in a way, to the individual.

Insofar as religion is concerned:

. . . the secularism that pervades the American consciousness is essentially of this kind: it is thinking and living in terms of a framework of reality and value remote from the religious beliefs simultaneously professed. . . .

This is at least part of the picture presented by religion in contemporary America: Christians flocking to church, yet forgetting all about Christ when it comes to naming the most significant events in history; men and women valuing the Bible as revelation, purchasing and

---

[3] C. E. Ayres, *Towards a Reasonable Society* (Austin: University of Texas Press, 1961), pp. 291-294.

distributing it by the millions, yet apparently seldom reading it themselves. Every aspect of contemporary religious life reflects this paradox—pervasive secularism and mounting religiosity, 'the strengthening of the religious structure in spite of increasing secularization.' The influx of members into the churches and the increased readiness of Americans to identify themselves in religious terms certainly appear to stand in contrast to the way Americans seem to think and feel about matters central to the faiths they profess.[4]

I do believe, contrary to what the increase in houses for worship might suggest, that institutionalized religion in America is giving way, more and more, to religion-as-an-individual-matter, and that it will eventually be replaced by social-humanitarian institutions of one form or another.

In family relations, most Americans practice democratic rule and each member of the family is encouraged to be on his own; as such, the family members tend to be independent of each other.

. . . The individual is seemingly allowed the utmost latitude in making his own choices—choosing his interests as he grows up, his companions and friends, his job and career, his mate, the size of his family, the color of his opinions, his recreations and hobbies, his books, his tastes, his residence. This degree of freedom of choice leads some observers to count America as the most permissive of societies.[5]

In relation to the nation, the individuals in America are not as yet independent as they are in relation to the church and/or the family. The individual is subjected to many restrictions in certain areas, especially in sexual relations and in particular for the girls. The formal codes of the American society are severely restrictive; however, the operative codes

---

[4] Will Herberg, *Protestant-Catholic-Jew* (New York: Doubleday & Company, 1955), p. 14.

[5] Max Lerner, *America As a Civilization* (New York: Simon & Schuster, 1957), p. 545.

are much less so. That is to say, there is quite a lag between the conceived and operative values of the society. As long as the individual does not get caught, he need not worry.

On the whole, this lag between conceived and operative values is on the way out. With the awakening of the young adults in the society, more and more of the restrictions are removed; thus, rendering the young adults more responsible, and as such, more free and independent.

This is the situation in America at present, but whether the Americans will make the "right" choice or not is all up to the education they receive and the mass communication they are exposed to. Responsibility in mass communication might turn out to be the determining factor in what the Americans are led to believe and in what they are led to act upon.

But, actually, in order for the Americans to make the right choice, the United States needs more than responsibility in mass communication. In order to make the right choice, the United States needs the best planning and cooperation that the international community can provide. Without international cooperation, I am afraid, the United States will remain a mere potential, torn between ideals and the immediate self-interest, with more and more room for alienation from the rest of the world, and more and more alienation of the individual American as well. In the past, alienation of the individual and defeatism on his part succeeded in undermining the greatness of the state and the civilization, and consequently led to a defeating war or organizational degeneration, both of which are potent weapons in the collapse of any civilization.

Freedom in America, as I have already indicated, is unmatched in any of the countries that I am familiar with, and in the Arab countries in particular, where there is no place for comparison. The degree of individual freedom I felt when I came to the United States was so overwhelming to me, that it took me some time to get used to it. In Jordan, where I lived the first eighteen years of my life, freedom does not exist. One is not free to do anything there.

In relation to the family, the individual in Jordan is almost absolutely governed by his parents. He is not allowed to make any choices for himself. He remains dependent on his parents for a very long time. Even at the age of eighteen, one is not able to make a choice; that is because, up to that age, all the choices had been made for him. If the choice is not made by one's parents, it is made by the older members of the family, by the school, by society, or by the government. The degree of control which the individual is subjected to in Jordan is unbearable. Whereas, here in the United States, the degree of freedom one is given is unbearable. This is the case especially when freedom is understood to exclude responsibility. When freedom is understood to *include* responsibility, and there is so much of it present, the individual might, at times, feel alienated by it.

American life, no doubt, falls short of the ideals that the Americans uphold. The Americans, however, are constantly fighting the gap and trying to reach those ideals. Because of their conception of freedom and the way freedom is exercised in America, progress towards the ideals is slow. But progress is present, nevertheless; and if the Americans are successful in maintaining a favorable balance in the "race between civilization and catastrophe," and if international cooperation is secured in this race, then the promise for the future could very well be, "from each according to his ability, to each according to his needs."

# CHAPTER III.

# Socialization of the Individual

Socialization refers to the process by which persons acquire the knowledge, skills, and dispositions that make them more or less able members of their society. It is apparent that the socialization experienced by a person in childhood cannot prepare him for all the roles he will be expected to fill in later years. People move through a sequence of different positions in society, in accord with different stages of the life cycle. Changes in the demands upon them arise from their mobility, both geographic and social, and from the customs of their society which may vary during their lifetimes.[1]

Socialization is the process by which a human organism is rendered a member of a certain society. That is, the organism is converted from its original animal state to its ultimate state of human being. Through this process, the organism becomes aware of the requirements necessary for it to function well in a particular culture. The ultimate state of the human organism is a function of: (1) a biological inheritance, (2) a geographic or physical environment, (3) a social environment, and (4) a cultural environment.

The biological inheritance of the organism determines to a great degree, its social life. The difference in the genes and/or sex gives the organism a different role and attitude, through most of its life span. "The biological factor is important in

---

[1] Orville G. Brim, Jr. and Stanton Wheeler, *Socialization After Childhood: Two Essays* (New York: John Wiley and Sons, Inc., 1966), p. 3.

man's social organization. The attraction and mating of the sexes, the relationship of mother and children, the long period of infancy and the helplessness of the child have made the family a permanent institution." [2] The color of the skin is another important biological factor in the socialization of the individual, especially where the color of the skin creates some sort of prejudice.

The geographic environment—climate, location, and natural resources—determine what personality traits are to be developed and what traits are to be inhibited.

> The physical environment has always been an important influence in bringing men together. Good soil, the protection of mountains and rivers, good resources in fish, game, minerals, and forests, have all caused men to seek favorable spots for settlement, from the primitive days of the flint bed to the modern oil reserves and rubber plantations. There can be no intelligent study of social groups which does not include a consideration of the geographical factor. [3]

The cultural environment determines the variety of skills and knowledge the organism acquires. And the social environment is very much related to the cultural environment. The values, both cultural and social, play a very significant role in the formation and molding of the personality.

"There are three main processes involved in socialization. The first is proper performance behavior or that behavior acceptable to society. Second, the playing of approved social roles. And third, the development of social attitudes." [4] The drive to be with people begins during the first year of a person's life. From this first year of life, a child tends to increase his social participation and, thereby, the amount of interaction increases. By trial and error, a child will learn some of the

---

[2] Harry E. Barnes and Oreen M. Ruedi, *The American Way of Life* (New York: Prentice-Hall, Inc., 1942), p. 47.

[3] Barnes and Ruedi, *The American Way of Life*, p. 47.

[4] Elizabeth B. Hurlock, *Child Development* (New York: McGraw Hill Book Co., Inc., 1956), p. 325.

behavior patterns necessary for good social adjustments. He may learn to get along with others by imitation, or through some other method of learning.

Though there are four factors mentioned above, this chapter will be mainly concerned with the social environment of the individual. This environment is dealt with in terms of the family, the church, the school, and other social and cultural institutions.

> The family is the basic unit of society. It is the most important primary group. It is also the oldest institution and has a basic influence in the socialization of the individual. It has become a more specialized agency for the socialization of children and the stabilization of adult personalities.[5]

As a primary group and as an institution, the family performs the general functions of reproduction or race perpetuation, protection and care of the young, conservation of culture, and provision of intimate contact. William F. Ogburn lists seven functions of the family. "These seven functions—economic, status giving, educational, religious, recreational, protective, and affectional—may be thought of as bonds that tied the members of a family together." [6]

In the United States, the function of the family, as I see it, is first, reproduction. The family is responsible for producing legitimate offspring. A second function of the family is protection of the offspring. Third, the family performs a socializing function. Fourth, the family performs an affectional-emotional function. Affection is primarily a characteristic of small groups, and the family is ideal for providing emotional security. A child must be loved; he must know that he is loved, and he must feel that he is important to someone else. Through family interaction, the child obtains this emotional-affectional security. The fifth function of the family is the regulative

---

[5] Paul H. Mussen, *The Psychological Development of the Child* (Englewood Cliffs, New Jersey: 1967), p. 68

[6] William F. Ogburn, "The Changing Family," *The Family* 19 (July, 1938), pp. 139-41.

function, which incorporates the relationship between the sexes, between parents and offspring, among siblings and regulates other relationships present in the family structure.

All the above functions are present in the American family to some degree. However, it may be claimed that only one of these functions remains as vigorous and extensive as in prior eras. The other functions have been reduced as family activities in recent times. Even the reproductive function is reduced also; many of the children born are mere accidents. As far as protection is concerned, although the family is the original unit, much of the burden has recently been shifted to extra-familial agencies. Also many of the socialization processes are either assumed by some extra-familial institution, or forfeited by the parents and delegated to such an institution. As far as the emotional-affectional security is concerned, neither parent is home often enough or long enough to provide this security. The children seem to be cared for by a baby-sitter most of their waking hours, and might even feel rejected by the parents. The regulative function seems to be completely reduced. Because of the minimal interaction between the parents and the offspring, the family regulations would be least effective and tend to give way to regulation by the peer group, and thus the family is rendered more and more egalitarian.

There are a few other things I want to mention at this point in relation to the American family. The way the new family is set up in America makes possible a rare and incomparable degree of privacy to the two partners.

> No matter how hard it has been to arrange for privacy before marriage, as soon as the wedding is over, everybody expects them to have their own latch key and their own possessions around them. If they cannot manage this, they feel cheated and other people think something is wrong.[7]

Another important value the new family has is the free choice available to it. They are not only free from the dictates

---

[7] *The Family: Its Function and Destiny*, ed. by Ruth N. Anshen (New York: Harper and Brothers, 1949), p. 162.

of the parent-families, but they are also comparably free to move wherever they want, to choose their own friends and neighbors, and make their own budget. With some exceptions, they are also free to terminate the marriage if they are not compatible, just as they were free to start it.

With the loss or reduction of many of the family functions, the American family has unusual potential leisure. This leisure is made more concrete due to the many labor-saving devices available to the American family. Most of this leisure time is used up by the wife for things she thinks will keep her husband. She spends hours making herself look as lovely and enticing as possible. This seems to be a strange thing to do, especially in the American culture, where marriage is supposed to be the result of love and a long period of dating and familiarity.

Compulsory universal schooling in the United States adds to the leisure time of the family by freeing it of many duties to the children. For the most part of the day, American children are the responsibility of the teacher and not of the parents. With the spread of the nursery school over the country, younger and younger children get trained care outside the home, and the parents, especially the mother, are correspondingly relieved of such labor.

Another quality of most American families is their non-authoritarian character. This lack of strong authoritarianism goes well with the pragmatic philosophy which has worked so well for the Americans.

Recognizing the great diversity in American families, I still would like to posit a concept of *the* American family. This, perhaps, is an ideal construction in that it only emphasizes what is distinctive of families in the United States in comparison with those of other countries. The structure of the family is, more or less, universally the same. It is only in terms of the process that these differences exist.

With all the variations in American families, I would say that *the* American family is characterized as merely a form of companionship. This characteristic emphasizes the point that *the* American family is more and more bound by the interpersonal relationship of its members, as compared with the older traditional type of family which is bound by tradition, public opinion, and law.

The American family, with its varied historical heritage, with strands going back to almost all other countries and religions, is distinctive both in its rural as well as in its urban setting.

The environment of the pioneers paved the way for the democratic family. From the early days of America, women and youth were emancipated from subordination to the family and to the community as well. Though the early rural family didn't realize a great degree of democracy among its members, it had nevertheless progressed towards the realization of that concept.

Industry and urbanization provided the necessary conditions for the development of this distinctive democratic characteristic. These phenomena greatly promoted the equality among family members. The family, in the urban environment, ceased to be a unity of economic necessity. This change helped in further reducing the authority of the family head. The potential or actual employment of the wife and children emphasized their economic independence and led to new relations among the family members. With each succeeding generation, parental control over children decreases. But the economic factor is not alone in bringing this about. There are other factors that led to the condition of *the* American family today.

The ideology of *the* American family—democracy, freedom, and self-expression—played a major role in bringing about the reality of freedom and individualization of family members and their release from the strict dictates of tradition, public opinion, and moral law.

The ideology of *the* American family is the major factor in saving it from collapsing in the face of urbanization. The survival of *the* American family in the urban environment shows the ability of the American to adapt to and to live with change. This ability is but one of the fruits of progressive education and it is a good fruit as to the survival of the American civilization.

One may also argue that the American family is broken up. The father is usually working most of the time; the kids are in school; and the mother is either working or socially absorbing herself into organizational activities. There are many occasions when the children do not see either one of their parents. This type of family makeup has left the children on their own. Many times they do what they please even when they should not. But who is to stop them when their parents are nowhere nearby? If the children are this way, they do not receive the discipline they should when they commit a wrong act. The more bad acts a child can get away with the greater the chance that his morals will decline more and more each time. This lack of discipline could explain the increasing crime rate and the decline of the social morals. In describing suburbia, Robert C. Wood says that:

> Suburban institutions are monuments of a society in which each member is attuned to the others but never to himself. The school emerges as the all-important focus of existence, and from the school, to children and parents alike, comes the constant message of "life adjustment!" As "opinion leaders," teachers strive to inculcate cooperation, belongingness, togetherness. Courses aim at "socializing" the child through a process by which he learns specific skills at the same time that he is taught to use them only in an overtly friendly manner. Competition is subdued; so is individualism; the cry is for a common outlook, and the discipline is achieved by indirect measures of ostracism. The generalization has even been made that by the time he gets to college, a suburban student chooses his career in business administration or science, where there are human relations to be cultivated or where there are facts, but where there are never values.
>
> The aim of learning to get along with others, of advancing oneself only as a member of the group, infects, it is said, family life and leisure hours. The commuter-father is no longer the figure of authority; stern measures of discipline are not countenanced, and even if they were,

the father is not home enough to use them in the proper time and place. Although family life is "important," and love and constant association are expected, the means for holding the family together are obscure. It is left to the mother and the schools, and the experts on whom both rely, to rear the child and run the suburb. Educated women, wanting motherhood but expecting something more, anxious to put their talents to use beyond the family circle, are in charge. Skipping from one meeting to another, indulging or wanting to indulge in extra-marital affairs, ceaselessly expunging their feelings of guilt by overprotecting their children, they rule suburbia. So the desires and demands of children—space for their play, their training, their future careers, their happiness—become the predominant force in suburbia.

The decline of individuality is also found, according to most reports, in adult associations and activities. Suburban friendships are determined, by and large, by the physical layout of the neighborhood in which they take place, or dictated by career maneuvering necessary in big organization office politics. In the politics of public life, suburbanites are passive consumers of the national issues of the day or "inside dopesters" on what the issues really are. On the local scene their political activity is frenzied but ineffective, for suburbanites are always ultimately manipulated by the shrewd, calculating developer, the old residents, or the school superintendent.

From this pattern of character, space, time and the interaction of these institutions and beliefs, most observers go on to say, has come a new type of culture. Self-consciously friendly, in constant association, afraid or unable to differentiate themselves from their neighbors, the suburban residents form a classless society. Suburbia is a melting pot of executives, managers, white-collar, successful or unsuccessful, who may be distinguished only by subtle variations in the cars they drive, the number of bedrooms in their house, or the tables they set. Their consumption is inconspicuous because they cannot deviate too far from the standards of their neighbors—but for the same reason it has a common quality. It is never ceasing, and for almost all suburbanites, time payments for purchases in an already overextended budget have replaced the "savings account.[8]

This quote is expressing the suburbanite's inability to leave his position in the social structure. Each member of the suburban class is just like his fellow suburbanite. People in suburban society develop friend relationships, but they do not attach any values to these relationships. They are living, but they know not for what reason.

[8] Robert C. Wood, *Suburbia—Its People and Their Politics* (Boston: Houghton Mifflin Co., 1958), pp. 6-8.

# CHAPTER IV

# Religion: Commitment and Compromise

In most societies, a person's status is ranked in a graduated series of steps of prestige. Where one stands on these steps depends upon one's growth, development, wealth, character, reputation, and mental and physical attributes. These characteristics are known as status symbols.

> . . . most of us surround ourselves, wittingly or unwittingly, with status symbols we hope will influence the raters appraising us, and which we hope will help establish some social distance between ourselves and those we consider below us.[1]

In modern times, religion is added on as another status symbol. Many people are affiliated with a particular religion because they believe that the association will assist them in gaining prestige. The foregoing is particularly true in the American society.

"The service and worship in the early church was plain and simple, consisting of prayer, Scripture reading, hymns and preaching."[2] The early Christians attended church to worship God; moveover, they were not concerned with social status: "All whose faith had drawn them together held everything

---

[1] Vance Oakley Packard, *The Status Seekers* (New York, 1959), p. 7.

[2] Walter Wallbach and others, *Civilization Past and Present* (Chicago, 1965), I, p. 202.

in common: they would sell their property and possessions and make a general distribution as the need of each required." [3]

In earlier days Protestant churches were institutions where brotherhood was predominant. The Protestant congregations were composed of members from virtually every segment of the entire community. However, today it is difficult to find a church that draws its members from the entire community. The tendency towards a more rigid class structure in Protestant churches is moving along with the "general trend" in that direction. This trend should not be too surprising, because Liston Pope has been quoted as saying, "Every American community . . . has some pronounced pattern of social stratification, and religious institutions are always very closely associated with this pattern." [4]

Going to church is a deeply felt, soul-searching experience for many Americans; however, many people attend church on Sundays because it is the action that is expected of "proper people." In this way they can be with a social group which they believe will add to their responsibility and social status. "And even those who take their worshipping seriously often prefer to do it while surrounded by their own kind of people." [5] Church affiliation is becoming less and less a soul searching experience of solemn worship. "For many people today, church membership means the opportunity to see the same people they meet at Kiwanis or the country club." [6]

In modern-day society "church belonging is formalized and has a tendency to become parallel, if not marginal to other social affiliations." [7] This trend becomes very obvious when we observe the youth of America.

> To most students the church is a community facility like the school, the drug store, the city government and the

---

[3] *New English Bible* (London, 1961), Acts 2:44, 45.

[4] Packard, p. 195.

[5] *Ibid.*, p. 195.

[6] Gibson Winter, *The Suburban Captivity of the Churches* (Garden City, New York, 1961), p. 161.

[7] Herve Carrier, S.J., *The Sociology of Religious Belongings* (New York, 1965), p. 191.

bowling alley. To them the church is a place where one goes to Sunday School, to young peoples meeting, to a church party; and to a small segment, it is a place to worship or to hear a sermon. It is not something special or supernatural as the minister and some elders would have them believe.[8]

Why do these young people bother with religion at all? The answer is a simple one. "Religion to these adolescents is comparable in a way to wearing clothes or taking a bath. It is something one has to have or do to be acceptable in society." [9]

Hollingshead found some very interesting information about church membership in his study of Elmtown's youth.

To be labeled a churchmember is very important, for it tells people where one belongs in the rather complex denominational structure. One can label himself a Methodist with approval and seldom, if ever, worship with the congregation; it is sufficient to be known as a member of an approved church. However if he blandly says that he is an atheist, barriers will be erected around him by the devout, for atheist and communist are two labels an Elmtowner must avoid if he desires to be accepted as a respectable member of society.[10]

Membership in Protestant churches and social status have a definite relationship.[11]

Further evidence that church membership is based largely on social status can be deduced from the following statement by Liston Pope, Dean, Yale University Divinity School: "Individual Protestant churches tend to be 'class churches' with members drawn principally from one class group." [12]

People today are not as concerned about the tenets of faith of the church. They are concerned about the social and eco-

---

[8] A. B. Hollingshead, *Elmtown's Youth* (New York, 1949), p. 246.

[9] *Ibid.*, p. 244.

[10] *Ibid.*, p. 245.

[11] Harry G. Dillingham, "Protestant Religion and Social Status," *American Journal of Sociology*, LXX (January, 1965), p. 416.

[12] Packard, p. 194.

nomic meaning of the particular church.[13] This fact is brought out in the findings of sociologist E. Franklin Frazier. Mr. Frazier reports that: "Some Negroes in professional occupations maintain two church memberships." They maintain their membership in the evangelical churches for business reasons (most of their clients are evangelicals) while "at the same time they affiliate with Episcopal, Congregational, or Presbyterian churches . . . because of their social status." [14]

Business meaning is a strong motivation for religious association. Benson reports:

> . . . Another motivation which prevails, especially in smaller communities, is that of businessmen seeking to establish themselves in the public view as morally upright and honest. Where church affiliation and attendance is made an informal test in primary group society of habits of character, regular church attendance is a necessity for a small-town businessman.[15]

Even among those who are not business and professional men, economic reasons rate high as a motivation for church affiliation.

> Since religion is in general, an indication of higher achievement and superior qualities of living, the practice and progression of religious beliefs and aims become attributes sought by people in their associates. . . . In social class ideology people believe that they succeed if they associate with those who are thought to be successful.[16]

A real influence in the estimation of class in England has been the religious and social differences between "Church and Chapel." The distinction still exists; furthermore, it has remained very meaningful until a short time ago. In the absence of information to the contrary, those in high positions

13 *Ibid.*, p. 196.
14 *Ibid.*, p. 199.
15 Purnell Handy Benson, *Religion in Contemporary Culture* (New York, 1960), p. 755.
16 *Ibid.*

are assumed to be members of the Church of England. If a person belongs to the Church of England, it is much easier for him to be accepted socially and receive appointment to office. "With the decline of non-conformity in recent years . . . the difference has become less sharp"; therefore, many in the upper strata of society are not affiliated with any church.

> Although militant Protestantism has declined and Roman Catholics and Catholicism are being accepted more readily, the Church of England still carries a great deal of prestige, and those who hope to climb the social-ladder need to sever other church connections and adhere to the established church.[17]

Class consciousness exists among various churches in America. Hollingshead, in his study of Elmtown's youth, found that:

> 91 percent of the students who claim affiliation with a local congregation are distributed among the different denominations almost exactly like their parents. In the adolescent group, as among their parents, the Federated attracted class II's, tolerates class III's, repels class IV's and has no class V's. The Methodist attracts class III's, tolerates class IV's and has no class V's. The Catholic and Lutheran parishes represent all classes, but the bulk of their membership comes from classes II and IV, and it is divided equally between these classes; both have twice as many affiliations from V as from class II. Like the Federated, the Baptist and Free Methodist are in a category by themselves; they are definitely class IV churches. They attract the class IV's, tolerate the class V's and repel class II's and III's. In the Baptist church, class III's and IV's play the same roles and occupy the same positions the class II's do in the Federated, but here they do not compete with them for leadership.[18]

In the class structure of churches in the United States, the Episcopal Church caters to the upper class. It has been noted

---

17 G. D. H. Cole, *Studies in Class Structure* (London, 1955), pp. 118-119.
18 Hollingshead, p. 249.

that wedding announcements in the *New York Times,* pertaining to families in the upper social strata had the ceremonies performed in the Episcopal Church. E. Digby Beltzel made a very interesting observation in his study of Philadelphian society. He found "that two-thirds of the Philadelphians who were in both the *Social Register* and *Who's Who* were Episcopalians." Many corporate, business, and social leaders favor the Episcopal Church over others because it is clearly related to the Church of England; the upper class in the United States has a tendency to favor all things British.[19]

As a person moves up the social ladder, the church services become more restrained, less emotional, less evangelical, and more intellectual.[20] A rector of an Episcopal church said that to the uneducated the Episcopal services may seem dry because the sermons are "literate," and then added: "The more churches become filled with the conservative and wealthy, the more reluctant they become to make faith relevant to all kinds of people." [21]

In many American churches that have a large number of wealthy upper class people, great care is exercised to limit the number of persons from the lower class from gaining membership in their churches. Two churches with the heaviest upper class membership "devised a method of limiting the number of persons from the lower parts of the class hierarchy" by establishing branches in the lower reaches of town that served as missions for people of the lower classes.[22] Furthermore, some churches have decided the best way to keep an exclusive constituency is to discourage those who apply for membership.

> A theological student reported . . . that when serving as an assistant in an upper-class suburban church he was advised by a minister to discourage applications for membership from those with lesser social status. He was told to do this by advising the applicant that he and his family would be happier joining a church where they had friends or where

19 Packard, pp. 196, 197.
20 *Ibid.,* p. 201.
21 *Ibid.,* p. 201.
22 W. Lloyd Warner and Paul S. Lent, *The Social Life of a Modern Community* (New Haven, 1941), p. 358.

they could find people with whom they could share things in common. If this discouragement failed, then the assistant was told to inform the applicant that he probably could not afford the amount customarily expected from members to defray church expenses. If none of these things worked then the assistant was to tell the applicant that there was a waiting list and that it would be a year or more before sufficient vacancies would occur for him and his family to be admitted. The minister said to his assistant, "We have a nice congenial fellowship, and we wish to keep it that way." [23]

Other churches favored by the two top social classes are Presbyterian, Congregational and Unitarian. In the choice of corporate executives, the Presbyterian church is second only to the Episcopal church. A Congregational minister in a midwestern town has been quoted as saying, "It has bothered me that we don't have a single farmer or workingman in the congregation." The numerically small Unitarian church has had more eminent Americans affiliated with it than has been associated with any other denomination.[24]

As we move down the social scale, we come to the denominations that have the largest following. The Methodist church is probably the choice of the average American. They are made up of the majority of the middle classes. A notch below them are the Lutherans. Somewhat below the Lutherans are the Baptists; however, in many communities, especially in the South, the Baptist church carries the highest prestige. The Baptist church is the church of the workingman.[25]

Studies have revealed that:

> . . . the percentage of Episcopalian, Congregational, Presbyterian, and Jews in upper-class income levels in business and having college degrees are approximately two or three times the proportion having these characteristics among Methodists, Lutherans, Baptists, and Catholics.[26]

23 Benson, p. 761.
24 Packard, pp. 198-99.
25 Packard, p. 200.
26 Benson, p. 759.

When religion begins to move toward the upper classes, new religious movements develop to meet the needs of the lower class persons. Examples of these movements can be seen in the Methodists and Baptists, and in recent years the Fundamentalists and Holiness groups. It is obvious that the Baptist form of church government would have less appeal to the emulous capitalist than the Presbyterian and Episcopal form of church government, and more attractive to the lower classes of society who desire to control their own affairs.[27]

At the bottom of the social scale are the Pentecostal and Holiness sects. These churches draw their constituency from the lower classes.[28] R. R. Dynes, in a study made in Columbus, Ohio, states that "churchness is strongly associated with high socio-economic status and sectness with low economic status." [29]

How do sociologists define a sect?

> By definition a sect is a group which consists of a small minority of people who follow a way of life which protests against that of the majority. Important examples of sects in American religious history are Christian Scientists, Jehovah's Witnesses, and Mormons.

In general, a sect is looked upon with disapproval by those who are not members of it. This results in the loss of social status in society; however, "at the same time those of lower social status may turn to sect-like religion as a means of self-expression and protest against those in power." [30]

Not only do the various denominations serve as status symbols, but there is a status to be gained or lost within a particular church.

> There is much . . . reference to religious symbols which include everyone in the democratic ideology of equality and fraternity among men and before God. However dif-

27 *Ibid.*, p. 760.
28 Packard, pp. 200-01.
29 Benson, p. 617.
30 *Ibid.*, p. 17.

ferentialism still appears in the attitude of members of the various positions among themselves. Each member has one vote in the election of officers, but the one with the highest social status will exert the greatest power and influence.[31]

According to a study made by Lazerwertz, "there was positive relationship between status and church attendance" within each denomination studied.[32] People do not only strive for social status by affiliating with a particular church, but they strive for recognition within the particular group with which they are associated.

In modern-day society, religion is a status symbol. A. B. Hollingshead has aptly said, "The churches too are placed in a prestige hierarchy." He has gone on to say that the "society church" is placed at the top of the social ladder with the holiness and pentecostal sects at the bottom.[33] All of the foregoing appears so strange in the light of the Scriptures:

> You are no longer Jews or Greeks or slaves or free men or women, but you are all the same—you are Christians.[34] In this new life one's nationality or race or education or social position is unimportant. Such things mean nothing; whether a person has Christ is what matters, and He is equally available to all.[35]

In a society where religion is reduced to a mere status symbol and where prestige and status take the place of religion, it is logical and practical to assume that commitment is dead, and that compromise and ambiguity take the place of commitment.

"It is obvious to any American that our whole national life is built on compromise, and that the great institution, the American Constitution, from which we suck the strength of

---

[31] W. Lloyd Warner, *The Status System of a Modern Community* (New Haven, 1941), p. 33.
[32] Dillingham, pp. 419-21.
[33] Hollingshead, p. 68.
[34] *Living Letters* (Wheaton, Ill., 1962), Galatians 3:28.
[35] *Ibid.*, Colossians 3:11.

our public life, is in itself a series of compromises, great and small. . . ." [36] This statement by Biddle on the American society was further generalized by Morley when he said, "All government, indeed every human benefit and enjoyment, every virtue, and every prudent act, is founded on compromise and barter." [37] Yes, it appears as though, in our American society, to exist is to compromise. But if this be the case, what of commitment? Cannot a person have convictions? Can he not be so committed to his convictions that he will not compromise and yet maintain existence in our society? It was said by John Morley in his essay *On Compromise,* "He who begins life by stifling his convictions is in a fair way for ending it without any convictions to stifle.[38] How and when, if ever, must compromise forego commitment? The design of this chapter is not to give the answers to this and other related questions, but simply to bring to the reader's attention some of the more prevalent issues on compromise and commitment and possibly further develop his understanding of them.

Truly in the Ameircan society, it appears that compromise plays an important and definite role. On the national level, in politics, the leaders seem to be faced with decisions, with arguments, with controversies, all of which are likely to evolve into some type of compromise, rather than a solution. To solve a problem is to find the answer to that problem. The mere word "compromise" connotes and denotes a giving-in or a concession on the part of both sides of the issue. To concede is to acknowledge and admit the truth of whatever it is one is conceding to. One can readily conjecture that in any compromise there is not a complete concession on either party. Thus, the problems may have been settled by compromise, but not solved by it.

To solve a problem one must first be aware of the existence of the problem in all its forms, shapes, sizes, and names. To find the best of all possible solutions, one must hear, know,

---

[36] Francis Biddle, "Necessity of Compromise," *Integrity and Compromise,* ed. by R. M. MacIver (New York: Harper & Brothers, 1967), p. 1.

[37] John Morley, *On Compromise* (London: Macmillan and Company, 1891), p. 228.

[38] *Ibid.,* p. 91.

and understand all the possible answers that we as members of the society can conceive. Only after a thorough analysis of the problem and its possible explanations can one make an intelligent decision as to which solution or combination of solutions would be more likely to solve the problem.

The masses of American society are being heard more today than during any other period. Because of the high degree of freedom of expression and assembly, they experience protests, sit-ins, strikes, marches, etcetera.

There are groups for and groups against practically any issue mentionable. Through the highly improved communications and transportation systems, every member of the American society is reached. Yes, the Americans can be and are being heard. But are they saying anything worth listening to? To quote John Morley again, "Ours, as has been truly said, is a time of loud disputes and weak convictions." [39] Because of their weak convictions, Americans are easily swayed from one extreme to the other, especially if the one they are hearing is "known" one way or another. This brings us to another important issue—that of commitment.

If we would sit and meditate as did Descartes, we would find ourselves doubting the existence of all things except perhaps the existence of our own intellect simply because of the fact that we can think. Descartes did not successfully find all the answers he was seeking, but he did make an attempt to find them. Pascal said on the subject of doubt, "He who doubts and searches not is a grievous wrongdoer, and a grievously unfortunate man." [40] One who seeks will find an answer. Whether his answer be valid cannot be determined immediately. However, the fact that the question is answered or that the problem is solved cannot be known simply because one person has sought and found. That person must next be committed to what he finds or to his beliefs. If he feels he has truly found an answer, he will be committed—completely.

"The question whether we can get others to agree with us is not relevant . . . the fact that others do not yet share our

---

[39] Morley, p. 129.
[40] Ibid., p. 131.

opinions, is the very reason for our action. We can only bring them to agree with us, if it be possible on any terms, by persistency in our principles," [41] said Lord Morley. Would the American society be as advanced as it is today if men like Henry Ford had not said and believed that he had a method of building a cheaper automobile. Or if no one in the fourteenth century stood up and proclaimed and proved the world was round, would there be an American Society? These examples are rather crude but they will illustrate the point that unless one desires to live in a passive and apathetic society, one would have to continue in the steps of the great men in the past. One would have to be committed wholly and sincerely, to his ideals.

You may ask why, if in the past the Americans have prospered and advanced, should they not continue accordingly? Lord Morley in the beginning of his essay affirms this when he stated, "the slovenly willingness to hold two directly contradictory propositions at one and the same time is coming more and more common." [42] This certainly is very true today. It is one of the major factors leading to apathy. He also said, "the devotees of the current method are more concerned with the pedigree and genealogical connections of a custom or an idea than with its own proper goodness or badness, its strength or its weakness." [43] This is the procedure followed in the writing of books and scholarly papers at the University level. What is a paper without the proper number of footnotes? The basic reason for this is that the American Society is a truly thriving society, boasting one of the highest economic levels in the world. Morley says of this, "this is the only catastrophe, in one of its many shapes of fatal doctrine that money, position, power, philanthropy, or any of the thousand seductive masts of the pseudo-expedient, may carry a man away from love of truth and yet leave him internally unharmed." [44]

But where is the "happy medium?" Where is the compro-

[41] *Ibid.,* p. 225.
[42] *Ibid.,* p. 18.
[43] *Ibid.,* p. 31.
[44] *Ibid.,* p. 93.

mise between compromise and commitment: As stated before in this chapter the American society is founded on compromise. If they were to be all committed completely to their own ideas, making no compromises whatsoever, the society would not be. Likewise, if they were to compromise with anyone about anything without any regard to their beliefs and their commitments, again the society would fail because it would have no grounds on which to stand. Both compromise and commitment are essential, but to what degree and in what areas is the question?

As has been previously stated, this chapter is not intended to give explicit answers to any issue, rather its purpose is to bring to the reader's attention some of the problems and issues with respect to compromise and commitment. It would be virtually impossible to cover every field in which compromise and commitment are of importance, and even more so to cover every aspect of each field. Thus I will narrow the discussion to some examples in the areas of politics, religion, science, art, and philosophy, giving brief, general, coverage to each field.

Politics in the American society seems to be less commitment and more compromise. The very fact that some Americans choose one of the two major parties over the other is a compromise. It would be unreasonable to say one party has a better policy on all points concerned than the other party. Eugene McCarthy said of compromise, "Compromise is the mark of human relations, not only in politics, but in almost every institution or social relationship involving two or more persons. Genuine compromise is not a violation of principle, not a compromise with principle, but with reality." [45] It is the politician's duty to compromise. A politician's commitment is not usually what suffers in a discussion of whether to compromise or not, but his conscience bears the burden. The dilemma of a politician was summed up by McCarthy when he said, "politicians are expected to be compromised, to compromise, yet they are ordinarily criticized for being compromisers." [46]

---

[45] R. M. MacIver, *Integrity and Compromise* (New York: Harper and Brothers, 1957), p. 19.

[46] *Ibid.*, p. 19.

In the area of religion one would expect an almost complete commitment with very little compromise. This is basically true. A religious man must be committed completely to his religion. This, however, is disputed by many who are converted from one faith to another upon marriage. It is also disputed by many who claim to be religious and try to prove it simply by going to church.

Many times a scientist will be much more committed than even a religious man. One reason for the scientist's firm belief was stated by Lord Morley when he said, "A person who takes the trouble to form his own beliefs and opinions will feel that he owes no responsibility to the majority for his conclusions. If he is a genuine lover of truth, if he is inspired by the divine passion for seeing things as they are, and a divine abhorrence of holding ideas which do not conform to the facts, he will be wholly independent of the approval or assent of the persons around him." [47] A scientist is committed yet he must compromise. A decision to try a certain plan of attack on an unknown area is a compromise by the pure scientist. The decision of a physician to tell a person the truth about the fatal disease or to lie to that person is a compromise of conscience and commitment. The decision of a scientist to turn over his knowledge from goodwill to destruction during a wartime situation would, along with these other compromises be an extremely difficult one to make. Because the scientist is so committed to his cause, his compromises seem to be of a larger magnitude and a higher degree of difficulty to execute than are those made by the ordinary man.

In speaking of art, there are two major aspects to consider. One is the commercial artist, the artists who illustrate magazine articles and advertisements. These artists must compromise in order to maintain their jobs. They are told what to illustrate, with the manner in which they do so left to their personal discretion. The other, for lack of a better word, shall be called the art-artist. He is the one who feels art is a true confession and this confession can be seen in his works. Al-

---

[47] Morley, p. 201.

though such art-artists are committed to art, there are very few who can afford (financially) to fulfill this commitment without the aid of another form of income. Thus they must compromise with what they desire to do and what they have need to do. Although an artist's work is beautiful and unique in his eyes, very few potential admirers will find a suitable compromise between the artist's work and their own ideas of a beautiful and unique piece of work. Thus an art-artist's life is full of disappointments if his goal is material wealth and well being. But if he is fully committed to his expression of art, he can someday look back on his works and say there had been no compromises.

From the above general examples, one can easily deduce that the areas of compromise and commitment are extremely complex and are quite relative to the field being considered. As each of us considers the importance of compromise and commitment in our lives let us keep in mind our ultimate goal and initiate the necessary conditions to successfully fulfill that goal. In considering which course to take in our own lives it would be well to remember Morley when he said, "The disciples of the relative may afford to compromise. The disciples of the absolute, never." [48] The Americans, being the disciples of the relative, make their life a total compromise.

American pragmatism wears many masks. It is the outgrowth and the result of the history of the country that spawned it, and it is a reaction or answer to the traditions that preceded it. The Puritan heritage still had a dominant position in American sentiment, and the extreme reaction of the deist was the opportunity for this philosophy to develop as a middle ground between these two extreme positions. I mean extreme in their relationship to each other. It attempted to bridge the gap between science and rationalism; between idealism and empiricism. It relied more heavily for its foundations on an appeal to empiricism, but it rejected the idea that pure perception was all that was relevant to the human condition. It introduced value on a new level, cognizant of the fact that J. S. Mill was

---

[48] *Ibid.,* p. 56.

unable to introduce it into Utilitarianism. It was sympathetic to the utilitarian view. Value became individual incidents rather than universal facts. Pragmatism as a philosophy was introduced by Charles Pierce strictly as a better way to cope with science. William James introduced psychology as a factor in its development, and John Dewey attempted to apply it to a society trying to cope with the problem of a growing rift between science and the rest of society. It was an attempt at a new system of valuation which had its basis in reality and in experience, rather than in ideal and universal concepts.

Pragmatism studies the relationship of what is said about an experience, and what that experience actually is. It tries to eliminate contradictions in these two areas. It attempts to bridge the gap between the dualism of mind and experience. If a statement doesn't coincide with an experience or group of experiences the statement must be revised. Different pragmatists see the problem differently. Pierce would say that if the statement doesn't coincide with the experience it should be rejected. It makes no sense. In this he is the forerunner of the logical positivists who felt that a statement that steps beyond the bounds of human experience, should not be dealt with. In one step eliminating all ontological arguments. William James would approach the problem in a different way. He didn't wish to eliminate God from his view of the world. He expanded on Pierce's position that the effect of a thing was the belief that it caused, and that these beliefs become habits. James introduces a more utilitarian concept in asserting that a true statement is a statement that results in satisfaction which results in belief. Even James' ontological position was skeptical using the foundation of satisfaction as its criterion. Dewey tends to solidify and expand the theory of Pierce that habit is the true criterion of value. He expands it from a personal to a more social concept, and sees social problems being resolved through this method. He also feels that thought and decision play a larger part in deciding value than does experience.

Action is a key to the pragmatic philosophy. Thought and function become simultaneous and inter-related. The world may be made up of ideas or of experiences, but they have no meaning beyond how they relate to man. Man is constantly beset with problems in dealing with the world around him. How he solves these problems determines the amount of satisfaction and ease in which he can live in the world around him. Each time he solves a problem new problems arise, but there is no reason to believe that he cannot solve these new problems and regain his sense of satisfaction. Pierce goes so far to say that an eventual application of these principles could result in a final solution to all problems. Dewey would not consider a development toward final solutions a viable position. He is concerned only with what the man meets at each step. A major point that must be re-emphasized, which runs through the philosophy of all these men, is that beyond a practical application all thought is less than valuable. All the polemics of philosophy have no meaning if they are unable to solve practical problems. This neatly eliminates ontological speculation as a viable form of thought.

Freedom is not as important a concept in pragmatic philosophy. When one attempts to solve a problem it is a problem that already exists, and to speculate on what might have been is useless unless it can be practically applied to some future circumstances. The will, which is the stimulus of freedom, also has less of a place in this philosophy. It provides the impetus for action, but beyond that it falls into the category of the speculative. Behaviorism plays a strong role in pragmatism. Until a problem occurs it cannot be worked out, and once it occurs it is no longer in the realm of will or freedom.

Herein lies the responsibility. All action involves all people around us. We are responsible for our actions because our actions involve others. Man is involved. The difficulty lies in the degree of involvement. There is a certain valuation in ascertaining this degree. This is partially accomplished by considering the limitations of any action, or the possibilities, beyond which, it would be foolish to speculate. One cannot get involved with ideologies of a distant people. For how can one assume knowledge of the conditions that arose which fostered these ideologies. Without the common bond of belief in human nature or the universal qualities of a certain group of ethics how can you commit yourself? If you don't, what are you left with? You are left with a philosophy of non-involvement. Freedom, of course, leaves one to act as he must, but act he must. Action always extends beyond the boundaries one sets for it. Involvement always traps us. History is penetrated with accidents. Accidents are generally caused by stepping beyond one's self-imposed limits.

Let me end this chapter with a quote from the introduction to Walter Bagehot's *The English Constitution,* by the First Earl of Balfour:

> It matters little what other gifts a people may possess if they are wanting in those which, from this point of view, are of most importance. If, for example, they have no capacity for grading their loyalties as well as for being moved by them; if they have no natural inclination to liberty and no natural respect for law; if they lack good humour and tolerate foul play; if they know not how to compromise or when; if they have not that distrust of extreme conclusions which is sometimes misdescribed as want of logic; if corruption does not repel them; and if their divisions tend to be either too numerous or too profound, the successful working of . . . institutions may be difficult or impossible.[49]

---

[49] First Earl of Balfour, "Introduction," *The English Constitution,* by Walter Bagehot (Oxford University Press, 1928), p. xxii.

# CHAPTER V

# Discrimination in the United States

## INTRODUCTION

All the Americans are involved. Many of them cringe with resentment when they hear words like discrimination, segregation and civil rights. The news media have tired of the subject. However, the poor light cast on racial problems by television doesn't lessen the magnitude of their importance.

"Discrimination can take the form of many wide and varied forms. Similarly the definition may assume diverse meanings. . . . For our purposes, discrimination is the application of standards which are arbitrary and unfair by major social standards." [1]

In a society in which great emphasis is placed on the possession of money as a means of getting as much out of life as possible, those who have acquired this necessary means are understandably interested in maintaining the conditions which make possible the continuance of the system. If the oppression of any minority group is involved in this process, it may at once be justified on the grounds of a thousand rationalizations.

It is becoming increasingly apparent that with an increase in international mass communication, America's position as a leader is becoming challenged due to deviations from her democratic creed.

Segregated and unprivileged groups have gained a great

---

[1] Ashley Montagu, *The Humanization of Man* (The World Publishing Co., Cleveland & New York, 1962), p. 213.

deal of power in the last generation; power with which to fight much more effectively than in the past for equality of opportunity. The increase in education, income, political participation, and in the effectiveness of their protest organizations make Negro Americans and other minorities better able to attack the walls of segregation. The aftermath of Dr. Martin Luther King emphasized that now is the time for change in the race relations within the United States.

Communism, once avowed to take the world by force, is now content to sit by and watch the opposition destroyed from within. If we as Americans do not act with responsibility and haste, we may see our ruin. Some so-called realists plead, "desegregation cannot happen overnight," but it will and the smoother the transition to an integrated and racially free state, the better off we all are. Granted, there is a fine line between pluralism and racial injustice, but there is yet much to be done before towing the line.

Still resisting changes are those afraid of financial loss. In many cases, this fear has been statistically proven to be needless. Answers to questions like "Will my customers stay away if I hire a Negro clerk?" "Will my employees work beside him" are invariably yes. In fact completely open hiring policies reduce labor costs. There are some risks but usually only in the short run.[2]

There is overwhelming evidence that if Negroes are from equivalent background and experience they will perform as well as white persons. Out of this fact arises two problems. First, many people tend to judge everyone by their own cultural experience thinking that theirs is inherently superior. Mass communication has helped to a small extent to lessen the amount of social difference. However, mass communication offers as many problems as it cures. Minority groups of low economic status become dissatisfied by being continually exposed to an upper middle-class standard of living. Some support the contention that mass communication is lessening individual thought and causing regimentation. Secondly, many

---

[2] Isador Chein, "Some Considerations of Intergroup Prejudice," *Journal of Educational Psychology.*

minority group members have never had the opportunity of educational experience available to most white families. Therefore they have created a culture within a culture far removed from the original.

Here again we are faced with a problem of values. A person may boast of liberalism claiming to be without prejudice yet defend to death his right to choose his neighbors. If we examine socially accepted institutions like private schools which segregate according to religion, we find that this argument doesn't seem without base. Issues that are founded on differing values are the most difficult to solve. There are, however, some dimensions of prejudice that can be approached with likely solutions. For example, when a person or group of persons is prejudiced due to a stereotyped view of the minority, personal contact may in some instances be effective. The major modification of this idea remains that equal status contact across group boundaries is the most likely to succeed in friendly inter-group relations. When a doctor meets a dentist, when a bricklayer meets a pipe-fitter across racial boundaries, prejudice and hostility are most likely reduced. There are, however, a number of questions that need to be asked. Does contact among those of an equally deprived status have the same effect as contact among those of an equally privileged class. Also, there is a danger that such contact will be somewhat contrived or artificial, that it will obscure some of the hard facts of life in America. Here and elsewhere, a little learning is a dangerous thing. If you seek to participate effectively in reduction of discrimination you will need a tough-minded realism about human relations, not a few polite encounters in the college classroom.[3]

Also, if a person carries false prejudices they may be weakened by education. The term education here is meant in a very broad sense. People act sometimes against prejudices in a nondiscriminatory way thus hiding their prejudice. Therefore, the only way a person could reach them is through the indirect approach. It is a well-known fact that if you try to

3 Robert K. Merton, *Social Theory and Social Structure* (New York: 1957), chapter 8.

argue someone out of a point of view, he is likely to argue back, to defend himself, to search for good reasons why he believes what he does. But if you change the circumstances of his life within which that point of view prospered and then offer him alternative ways of defining the situation, his prejudice is more likely to decline.

Often ignorance is not completely due to a lack of information but merely due to convenience. By removing this convenience or by changing the economic situation, for example, we may educate in the true sense of the word. It may help to create a situation in which the convenience of ignorance having been reduced, more persons can afford to listen.

Education has been hallowed by many writers as the answer to our racial problem. However, there is a danger of expecting too much of education. For example, education can only prosper in a supportive atmosphere.

The attitude of the upper classes toward the Negro is different in some respects from that of the lower classes. There is more hatred for the Negro among the lower classes because they consider him an economic threat to their own security, at least they have been taught to consider him so. In the South, the most vigorous opposition to desegregation comes from areas of economic stagnation and declining population. It is precisely those who belong to these groups that are under the most severe pressure and therefore most likely to express intergroup hostilities, who are least likely to be reached by any direct educational venture. Education that misses many strategically important people is only of secondary importance. For this reason those who are interested in reducing prejudice and discrimination must give some part of their effort to the task of relocating those in the dominant group who are under severe pressure. Only when some of the most severe threats have been removed, when life holds some promise of dignity and security, will those who are now filled with bitterness and frustration be ready for change.

An application of this strategy may be cited where the Blackstone Rangers from the Negro ghetto of Chicago were encouraged and given the opportunity for dignity by becoming a singing group. Once a severe threat to most Chicagoans, the group is appearing on national television singing themes appropriate for their cause.

When members of any group see no way out of their difficulties, when they feel utterly helpless, they are liable to accept symbolic schemes that promise them relief and a sense of meaning. They become "true believers." And their belief may be in complete superiority of their race, religion, or nation. By promoting an environment where their political voices can be heard, where job security can be found, where they have some say in their work situations, one supports a situation where they are ready for education and for the learning of new ideas of race relations.

Up to this point the discussion has been limited to changes necessary by the white majority. Generally speaking the more severely unprivileged the minority, the more responsibility there lies on the white majority for change. However, as the situation improves, as it has in many communities, the emphasis should be switched to the Negro. There often exists a lack of ambition, responsibility, or lawfulness that can be seen as natural results of segregation and persecution. The lower class American Negro is oriented to an authoritarian power structure. When this power structure collapses many are ill-equipped to handle the situation. As one Negro put it when asked about advice he would give his son in view of a newly passed fair employment law with which he was unfamiliar: "No need to get an education. You can't fight them big wheels." [4] Some of the effects of such an attitude, conveyed to children in many ways through the years are high drop-out rate from school, failure to enroll in technical programs that lead to higher paying jobs, and entrance to low-pay, low-prestige occupations that serve to reinforce the cycle in the next generation. Fortunately, this process is becoming less prevalent. What we must remember, however, is that those who are still frustrated are the cause of our racial problems and it is on them that we must concentrate.

---

4 Robert K. Merton, Chapter 8.

Nobody can deny the impact of the civil rights movement. Practically every newscast reminds us of racial tension. Often people get tired of even discussing it, thinking the subject overworked or impossible. However, there is hope for future equality and racial rest. We must not let the news of violence on the streets shock us into useless hate. We as educators hold more responsibility for the future of our nation than most people.

In a nation that is research-oriented, spending millions on the space program every year, little effort has been made to research the social ills of our country. Oftentimes social research is less obviously fruitful than research of a physical nature, but far more benefit would be gained by society if half the funds spent on space research were designated for the investigation of social problems.

Ever since the middle of the eighteenth century friendly visitors from other lands have remarked over and over again about the severe disabilities under which the American Negro lives. They have seen the treatment of this race as utterly contrary to the spirit of American institutions and American proclaimed ideals. This contradiction was eloquently summarized by Gunnar Myrdal, a distinguished Swedish social scientist, in his great two-volume work, *An American Dilemma*, published in 1944. He characterized the treatment of the Negro in the United States as the "greatest and most conspicuous scandal," as the "greatest failure." Moreover, he wrote, "the simple fact is that an educational offensive against racial intolerance . . . has never seriously been attempted in America." Here is a cancer eating at the heart of American democracy. It may well prove to be a vital factor in the triumph or defeat of the cause of freedom on the earth.

We must realize, and swiftly, that one of the most revolutionary changes taking place in the present epoch involves the relations of races and peoples. A great cycle, embracing approximately five hundred years, is closing in our day. In the middle of the fifteenth century the peoples of Europe seemed on the verge of being enslaved or driven into the sea. The Tartars still controlled much of Russia; the Moors were still entrenched in Spain; and the Ottoman Turks were striking boldly and successfully at the gates of southeastern Europe. Then, owing to a number of factors, including certainly the invention of new weapons of warfare and the advance of nautical science, the tables were turned. The peoples of Europe took the offensive and moved out in all directions from their cramped quarters. By the end of the nineteenth century they held nine-tenths of the land surface of the globe, dominated the remainder, and ruled the "seven seas." As a result of their fabulous successes, they developed a sense of unqualified superiority and assumed that they were destined by their own nature to govern the world. Today the colonial empires formed in the epoch of European ascendancy are in process of disintegration and the colored peoples are rising everywhere. That these peoples will be satisfied with anything less than equality of status among the nations is altogether improbable. And it must be realized that three-fourths of the human race are colored.

This situation throws the spotlight of history on the treatment of the Negro. The treatment of the Negro and all other minority groups provides the touchstone by which the integrity of the American people must be measured. For generations now they have freely and universally professed the commitment to the ideals of individual worth, human brotherhood, and equality before the law and in the moral order of the Judeo-Christian ethic and the democratic faith. These values are enshrined in the most sacred documents of the Republic— in the Declaration of Independence, the Federal Constitution, and the Gettysburg Address. Americans proclaim them to themselves and to the world on every occasion. In the measure that they show in their practices of prejudice, hatred, contempt, or discrimination toward any element of their people, they are weakened both at home and abroad, their full human resources are not developed, and the demagogue will be able to poison the political life. Also, in the measure that they are governed by the doctrines of racial, national, or religious superiority, their democracy will be corrupted at the core. They

49

shall know in their hearts that they are false to their professions.

As they look beyond their shores they see at once that the issue is not only domestic in character. They are engaged with the other nations of the free world in the daring and difficult venture of building an international organization designed to establish an enduring peace on the earth. If this organization is not to be despotic in character, it must rest on the principle of equality of peoples. Obviously, if Americans violate this principle at home, they can scarcely stand before the nations and fight in good conscience for the ideals of equal justice in the world. To the oppressed and underprivileged, to the colored and colonial peoples beyond their borders, to the men and women of good will everywhere, American actions at home will overwhelm their own words in international councils. And as the most powerful of the free nations they are supposed to guide other peoples down the road to freedom.

As Americans seek to lead the free world in the struggle against the ruthless thrust of Communist despotism, this question of American treatment of the Negro and other minority groups in the U.S. assumes a fateful urgency. With vast resources and fanatical energy the tiny oligarchy in the Kremlin is conducting a campaign of hate throughout the earth, and particularly in the regions inhabited by colored peoples, designed to convince all mankind that American democracy is a fraud. With a world-wide propaganda network under their direction these men note every American delinquency and carry it in greatly exaggerated form to all countries. Among other things they say that "in America, the Negro is not regarded as a man," that "there is no penalty for beating a Negro or raping a Negro woman," that this is a "right protected by law and forgiven by the church," that "lynchings and pogroms are very widespread in the United States," that "with persons subjected to lynching it would be possible to populate a huge city." Obviously Americans must strive steadfastly to remove from their common life everything that lends the slightest support to this violent campaign of misrepresentation.

It is in this broad context of American moral commitments

50

and the American position in the world that Americans should consider the decision of the Supreme Court of May 17, 1954 on the abolition of racial segregation in the schools. That this was a glorious decision and an authentic expression of the finest American traditions is clear to all thoughtful men and women. It served to ease the troubled conscience of many an American citizen. Also it served to discomfit the totalitarian adversary in all parts of the world. Indeed it was the most powerful blow struck by America in the current struggle for the minds and hearts of men.

The decision of the Court is only the first step on a long journey. Racial prejudices and hatreds still exist in America; and they are as real as rivers and mountains. They will consequently be removed only as Americans, as individuals and groups, rise to the highest levels of conscience, understanding, and resolution. Although the rule of law is one of the greatest achievements of Western man, there is that vast domain outside the law in every free society which Lord Moulton has called the realm of the "unenforceable," in which conscience rules. "Obedience to the unenforceable" is the moral foundation of a good society.

Unfortunately the President of the United States at the time remained silent on this great issue for a long time. And when he did speak, it was altogether too little and too late. Here was one of the greatest and most tragic failures of leadership by an administration that has chronically refused to lead in both domestic and world affairs. As early as February, 1956, the Liberal Party challenged the President to make his position unmistakably clear and in the name of the American tradition of equality, justice, and liberty to appeal to the conscience of Americans on this supreme moral issue. He chose to leave the matter to others and thus abdicated his responsibilities as the official spokesman of the nation in favor of Faubus, Almond, and the violent wing of the segregationists. The "American Dilemma" of Myrdal is fast becoming an "American tragedy." [5]

---

[5] Adapted from an unpublished speech by Prof. George S. Counts.

# DISCRIMINATION AND THE NEGRO

"There is no doubt that after the Civil War, Congress intended to give the Negro "social equality" in public life to a substantial degree. Besides the Thirteenth, Fourteenth, and Fifteenth Amendments to the Constitution (known as the Reconstruction Amendments), there was the Civil Rights Bill of 1875, which was explicit in declaring that all persons within the jurisdiction of the United States would be entitled to the full and equal enjoyment of inns, public conveyances, theaters, and other places of public amusement." [6] Negroes, however, met segregation and discrimination even during the few years of equality. In 1883, the Supreme Court declared the Civil Rights Bill of 1875 unconstitutional.

Negro conditions in some ways became worse than they had been under slavery. Now every man's hand was against him. If he owned property, he was likely to be cheated out of it. If he walked on the streets he was in danger of being kicked or stoned. If he had a job, he dare not quit or ask for a raise in pay. If he took his problems to the court, he was thrown out. If he fought back, he was lynched.

After the Civil War little one-room schools houses in which classes were taught to Negro children were burned in the South and Southerners made life miserable for Northern teachers who came down to help the freedman. Florida and Kentucky passed laws making it a crime for a white person to teach a Negro.

The Jim Crow legislation in Southern States and cities separated groups in schools, railroad cars and streetcars, in hotels and restaurants, parks and playgrounds, in theaters, and public meeting places. Jim Crow laws treated Negroes somewhat differently, depending upon their class and education. In the South today, survival of slavery socially exists where friendliness is restricted to the individual and not to the group. When the Negro rises socially and is no longer a servant he

---

[6] Arnold Rose, *The Negro in America* (Boston: The Beacon Press, 1959), p. 191.

becomes a stranger to the white upper class. "Nigger" and "darky" are even used in his presence, though it is well-known that Negroes find these terms insulting.

Many Negroes, particularly in the South, are poor, uneducated, and deficient in morals and manners, and are not very agreeable as social companions. In the South, the importance of this is enhanced by the great proportion of the Negro to the total population. Feeling still prevails that it will take several centuries for the Negro to be educated, cleaned, moralized, and made reliable. One Alabama politician put it this way: "No Negro in the world is the equal of the least, poorest, lowest-down white man I ever met." [7] There is a feeling centering around Negro inferiority and that Negroes like to be separated and are happy in their humble state and would not like to be treated equal.

Race prejudice is presented as a "deep-rooted, God-implanted instinct. This thought that Negro subordination is part of God's plan for the world has, however, never been uncontested." [8] Negroes were provided with an inadequate make-shift system of religious institutions. Social agencies undertaking work which the church never provided, faced the same problems. The Y.M.C.A. and Y.W.C.A. maintained separate branches for their work with the Negroes in the South. The Negroes in charge of these groups were not responsible for the situation since they had never been left the initiative in working among Negroes.

The Negroes were ridiculed in the press, on the platform, and on the stage.

In the Southern states they were taxed without representation. The poll tax featured the following: "1. Payment of the poll tax by others was made a crime. 2. Payment was required 6 to 10 months in advance of voting, when election was at its lowest point. 3. No special efforts were made in the states to collect the taxes; indeed the Alabama Constitution

---

[7] Milton Meltzer and August Mercer, *Time of Trial, Time of Hope* (Garden City, N.Y.: Doubleday and Co., 1960), p. 13.

[8] Rose, p. 193.

specifically forbade the use of any legal process to compel payment of the tax." [9]

It is difficult at present for one to realize that the first Negro riots occurred during World War I. The first major one broke out in E. St. Louis, Illinois, May 28, 1917. It lasted two days and two nights and did not end until martial law was finally declared. The second riot took place July 1, 1917, the most savage of all riots in which 500 Negroes were killed. Throughout 1917 riots broke out in such places as Camp Logan in Houston, Texas on August 16, 1917, for mistreatment of Negro civilians. Thirteen people were killed, all but one were white. "In savage reprisal which followed, thirteen Negro soldiers were executed—presumably a life for a life—and 41 were given life imprisonment." [10]

The Ku Klux Klan was reorganized in 1915. Tension increased. From June to December 1919 at least 25 riots took place. In later years riots would have led to meetings and attempts to solve problems which caused them, but instead the riots only increased segregation, hard feelings, and held back progress that could have come. From 1917-1921, there were 55 bombings of Negro homes in disputed neighborhoods in Chicago where 90% of the Negro population lived on the South Side.

Negro troops in World War I were not integrated with other units because of the policy and practice of the times. They were often stationed at the same place but facilities were segregated. This brought tension between white and Negro soldiers. The French treated Negro soldiers better than the Americans had treated them and some wondered if they should return home. This taste of equality was enough to arouse a desire for more.

Intermarriage has found both legal and social sanctions against it. "In 1787 an Indian Reservation in Virginia was accused of harboring an 'idle set of free Negroes.' It was

---

[9] Mill Maslow and Joseph B. Robinson, "Civil Right Legislation and the Fight for Equality, 1862-1952," *The University of Chicago Law Review*, p. 376.

[10] Carey McWilliams, *Brothers Under the Skin* (Boston: Little Brown and Co., 1951), p. 6.

pointed out that the proportion of Africans with Indian blood seemed to be about equal, for Indian women were married to black men and Indian men were married to black women." [11] About the same time slaves were escaping from Carolina and Georgia across into Florida where they were protected by the Indians. Interbreeding made it difficult to secure the runaway slaves. Sometimes when compelled to give up Negro women, the Indians refused to give up their children.

Manufacturing agents in the northern cities sent agents to the South to recruit Negro workers. Poems such as the following appeared in papers and expressed the Negro feelings of the day.

> Yes we are going to the North!
> I don't care to what state,
> Just so I cross the Dixon line
> From the southern land of hate.
> Lynched and burned and shot and hung,
> And not a word is said.
> No law whatever to protect
> It's just a "nigger" dead. [12]

The Negro soon found when he moved North in such great numbers that jobs become scarce, and problems of housing, education, and health became acute.

After World War II, Japanese-Americans returned to the West Coast but few Negroes returned to the South. The West Coast suddenly became the nation's new racial frontier. Negroes made more satisfactory adjustments in the rapidly growing cities in the West Coast than in any area they migrated. From 1940-1944, over 1,000,000 Negroes entered civilian employment. Skilled jobs doubled as did the number of single-skilled and semi-skilled. Colored workers entered industries, plants and occupations where few had been previously employed. By 1943, "hate strikes" were witnessed by many. Individual attitudes toward Negroes had changed as more and more Negroes moved into metropolitan industrial centers.

[11] Carter G. Woodson and Charles H. Wesley, *The Negro in Our History* (Washington, D.C.: The Associated Publishers Inc., 1966), p. 198.
[12] Meltzer, p. 20.

Lynching was no longer a chief threat against the Negro security, instead sadistic treatment by police officers. In 1951, 33 Negroes were killed while in police custody.

Businessmen have said that Negroes who move into white property depreciate it. This property is often disposed of at below cost. It is not the Negro causing the depreciation. History has shown that the Negro moving into property formerly occupied by whites, caused the landlords to receive larger incomes than before. The rent is often increased 15% to 30%. The Negroes were deprived of the right to move into city blocks where white people were in the majority, to purchase farm land in sections restricted to white ownership or to serve with whites in civil services. Some argued that desirable districts should be reserved for whites because lazy Negroes attached such a stigma to labor that whites would not work among them at certain occupations. The Negro, they further contended, had low standards of living; their wants were easily supplied.

"Seventy percent of whites agree that 'Negroes have less ambition than white people,' against 65% in 1966; 47% agree 'Negroes keep untidy homes' against 39% a year ago and 58% accept flat statements that 'Negroes have looser morals compared with 50% last year. The trend was the same on assertions that Negroes 'laugh a lot,' 'have less native intelligence,' 'Want to live off the handouts.' " [13]

The Negro has been discriminated against in voting up to the present time. Between 1938 and 1954, Thurgood Marshall took fourteen cases involving citizenship rights for Negroes to vote to the United States Supreme Court. In 12, he and his associates won favorable decisions. "But the crowning decision of the whole campaign was handed down on May 17, 1954, when the high court decided unanimously that segregation in public schools is unconstitutional." [14]

Discrimination still continues, but gains are being made through peaceful as well as violent means. In Montgomery, Alabama, Mrs. Rosa Lee Park, a young Negro woman, was

[13] "After the Riots; A Survey," *Newsweek*, 1967, p. 19.

[14] Arna Bontemps, *Story of the Negro* (New York: Alfred A. Knopf, 1960), p. 216.

arrested for not giving up her seat on a bus when ordered to do so. "Dr. Martin Luther King, highly educated and deeply Christian, expressed the feelings of the fight for Civil Rights when he said, 'They had chosen tired feet in preference to tired hearts.' " [15] The latest march to Washington and Resurrection City are another try at realizing the dream, "We hold these truths to be self-evident . . . that all men are created equal."

If nothing comes out of these peaceful demonstrations and marches, I think the situation will get much worse, and the American Society will speedily go down and pass away.

## DISCRIMINATION AND THE INDIANS

Today in the United States most attention to problems of discrimination is paid to the plight of the Negro, but there is an even older core of discrimination—discrimination against the indigenous population, the American Indian. For centuries the Indian has been ignored and pushed back into a corner of obscurity. How can this happen in America? Just exactly what kind of discrimination occurs against the Indians? Is anything being done to combat this?

Before we discuss the Indian and his problem, we should become better acquainted with the American Indian, his personality, and his way of life. At the time of the discovery of America, there were one million Indians living in what is now the United States. In North and South America there were around 30 million. Today of the 25-30 million Indians in this Hemisphere, there is a total of around 400,000 in the United States.[16] The million Indians who were in the United States and Alaska were formed into more than 600 societies—reservations—based on location, climate, and ways of life.

The entire life of the Indian was centered around his land. It was his food, his shelter, and his pride.

The factor of culture alone explains why Indians and white men, from the first days of European settlement,

---

15 *Ibid.,* p. 10.
16 Walter M. Daniels (ed.), *American Indians* (New York: The H. W. Wilson Co., 1957), p. 44.

have never reached a common understanding about land. The policy-makers of 1887 attempted to skip over centuries of historical growth by requiring Indians to become private landowners and to acquire the European psychology of individualism. It did not work out in the expected way, yet the policy makers of today still persist.

If an individual Indian owns a piece of land which controls the use of a larger area of adjacent land, the policy makers are encouraging that individual to act in a way that endangers the entire group—probably endangering his own status in the group. He is told that this is "the American way," and therefore the ideal way.

But there is an American way in these matters which is at least as old as the European feudal laws out of which private ownership gradually emerged. This older American way is entitled to work out its own process, which may or may not emerge as private ownership.

In the Indian concept, land is not "real estate." True, it has value; its products can sustain people. But first of all, in the Indian sense land stands for existence, identity, the place of belonging.[17]

Although before the white man's invasion, the Indians had unlimited warfare and lived dangerously, after the invasion they became even more warfaring and the Indian was made even more insecure. But this did not allow him to collapse. Pride and an unafraid, noble personality would not permit this.

> . . . the Indian went on, transmuting hard and faithless events into spiritual good. The Indian's spiritual and social hygiene remained triumphant. Pain beyond any possible telling, depopulation, the loss of homeland, the loss of any foreseeable future, all these he endured, and did not try to tell himself that they were less than they were. He kept his humor, his pride, his values of aristocracy, his power of love and his faith in gods who do not hate. Betrayed, overwhelmed, subjected to scorning hate, he was

---

[17] Harold E. Fey and D'Arcy McNickle, *Indians and other Americans* (New York: Harper and Brothers, 1959), p. 195.

never inwardly defeated. So the bleak record did not mean, to him, what it meant externally and what it must mean to you and me. Sadness deeper than the imagination can hold—sadness of men completely conscious, watching the universe being destroyed by a numberless and scorning foe—such sadness the tribal Indian knew through the long event. His spaciousness of life, the slow, immense rhythms of it, its tidal inflow and outflow of the boundless deep, and its spontaneity of joy which suffused the wise old, the earnest young and the child—these never failed.[18]

This spirit of the Indian can be seen later in history. President Theodore Roosevelt helped contribute a great deal to bringing the Indians into focus as they really were. Shortly before World War I President Roosevelt visited the Hopi peoples and extolled their way of life "as precious as anything existing in the United States." [19] When World War I came, and although the Indians were not then citizens and exempt from the draft, there were volunteers by the thousands which made a very widely acclaimed record.

At the beginning of the fight between the white man and the Indian, there was a somewhat liberal, curious attitude toward the Indians but through warfare there came to be an intense hatred and prejudice against the Indians.

After the day of rival imperialisms was over, however, there remained only one expanding empire, race-prejudiced and with a boundless land hunger. The former policies toward Indian societies and Indianhood became reversed; a policy at first implicit and sporadic, then explicit, elaborately rationalized and complexly implemented, of the extermination of Indian societies and of every Indian trait, of the eventual liquidation of Indians, became the formalized policy, law and practice.[20]

When looking at the outcome of just one specific tribe—

---

18 John Collier, *The Indians of the Americas* (New York: W. W. Norton and Company, Inc., 1947), p. 176.

19 *Ibid.*, p. 261.

20 *Ibid.*, p. 175.

the Shawnees—we can see how miserably the Indians were and still are treated. "They were being swept into that forced land-allotment designed to dispossess the pacified Indians and to wither their community life, which did in fact largely accomplish its end." [21]

Although the Indians proved that they could be a contribution to American society, as during World War I, they were constantly harangued and dealt with unfairly. The following are examples of this. The Indians began building a quite profitable cattle industry. They were eventually persuaded to sell their breeding stock and after a while the Plains tribes were pressured into turning over all lands into white leaseholds. Later a debate broke out when oil was discovered on Navajo land. It was finally decided "by law" that the oil was found on "Presidential decree" land and not that of the "Treaty" which would entitle the governor to control of the oil. At present, they cannot even invest their own money (which the U.S. Government holds for them) without permission from the Federal Government. All these anti-Indian acts can be attributed to Albert B. Fall, Secretary of the Interior, and his "legal" pressures to put the plans to work.

Another anti-Indian act occurred when the Fall administration sought the suppression of all native Indian religions still existing. This constituted the supreme attack against the Indians.

What could be left for an Indian—for any man—after his lands, his property, his religion, his way of life were declared illegal, which left him completely void of all rights as a man. How would a man react?

The Indians did not give up. They could not afford to become embittered and resentful. The Albert B. Fall administration was completely discredited and Fall himself was tried and imprisoned. His suppressions were overcome and through legal means, although almost against completely hopeless odds, the Indians were able to regain some of their rights. Indian title to some of the 16,000,000 acres of land was reinstated and

21 *Ibid.*, p. 181.

investigation was prompted in regard to Indian affairs. The tribes were counseled by some of the best legal and public affairs brains in the country. What follows are the principles as stated by the programs which were inaugurated in behalf of the Indians.

> These principles were: That Indians were entitled to the traditional American liberties, which included freedom of conscience, freedom of communication, freedom to organize politically and economically; freedom to use their assets productively, and to control them; access to the benefits of the general government (to which, indirectly and also directly, the Indians had contributed more of material wealth than any other population); and freedom to draw upon the wellsprings of whatever genius, fed from the mountains of whatever past, might be theirs.[22]

As can be seen from the preceding atrocities committed against the Indians, these things do happen in the United States, and not only to the Negro, as we sometimes have cause to assume. Hatred often takes many forms. One of my students has related to me the following: "Since I have lived in a rather Southern-attitude community, prejudice has often entered into my way of life—others who have not been involved in such a situation condemn those prejudices without looking at the motives. This is what I do in relation to the Indians. I condemn their adversaries from my point of view, but I do realize that some of the hatred felt toward the Indians can be justified. When I was very young, my family lived in South Dakota. The Indians were not even allowed to use the sidewalks, because their white neighbors considered them filth." Thankfully, something is being done about the Indian situation in America as can be seen by the reversal of Fall's blemishing acts. Education is going to be the turning point of this prejudice. Education has become the most desired element in Indian life, for the Indians realize that in order to fight the white man's disease of prejudice, they are going to have to be able to fight him on his own terms of intelligence and legality.

---

[22] *Ibid.*, pp. 258-259.

It is my opinion that to overcome prejudice of any kind, education will play a primary role. But this is a very slow process, and I am afraid it will take generations before the American Indian will feel free in his own country, his very own country.

## DISCRIMINATION AND THE MEXICANS, JAPANESE, AND CHINESE

Spanish-speaking people in the United States, 2,500,000 of them, make up what Dr. George I. Sanchey has termed "an orphan group," a forgotten people. Still largely unorganized and incoherent. The Spanish-speaking people constitute "the least known, the least sponsored, and least vocal large minority group in the nation." [23]

Mexicans are defined as born in Mexico or having parents in Mexico who are not definitely white, Negro, Indians, or Japanese.

What sets Spanish-speaking people apart, in addition to the fact that Anglos set them apart, is their identification with their environment. They migrated into the United States no farther than to environments similar to that of Mexico.

The status of the Spanish-speaking people has been affected often adversely by the state of relations between the United States and Mexico. The Mexican-American War left a heritage of ill-will and antagonism.

The language barrier, difference in religion and political institutions, and a host of important cultural differences, make for acute misunderstanding between Americans and Mexicans. These cultural prejudices trouble the poor when they apply for non-farm jobs for which they are qualified.

New Mexico and Arizona, being highly populated by Spanish-speaking people were denied statehood until 1912. The development of adequate public school systems in New Mexico was long delayed.

Labor has discriminated against Mexicans in an effort to protect living and working conditions by excluding them or

---

[23] McWiliams, p. 113.

by forcing them into undesirable jobs and by creating wage differentials. As such they are forced to live in slum conditions with poor sanitation, or in camps if they are migratory workers, where large families live in one-room shacks with no windows, no water or toilet facilities. Their condition is very similar to that of the Negroes. The Mexican and Puerto Ricans usually provide a buffer zone between the white and Negro neighborhoods.

The Japanese are essentially a middle-class or trading minority. They usually live in the same neighborhood.

The Japanese first came in large numbers during the 1890's as migratory agricultural workers. Many of them later became independent farmers, deep-sea fishermen or tradesmen. Hostility to the Japanese came mainly because the "small farmer" was able to raise crops on land where others had failed. Envy and covetousness resulted. In California, the Japanese controlled the local markets but could not enter out-of-state shipment business. Soon the out-of-state shippers eyed the local markets. In California, it was not until June, 1948 that alien Japanese could obtain commercial fishing licenses. In 1907, Japan had by a "Gentleman's Agreement" promised to prevent immigration of Japanese labor to the United States.

In 1906, the exclusion of Japanese students from the public schools of San Francisco raised a state-wide discussion and resulted in international negotiations between the United States and Japan. In 1903, the Anti-alien land laws were designed to prevent Japanese settlers from owning land. This caused much discussion and Secretary of State Bryan visited California in an attempt at forming a law acceptable to the people and yet not to disturb the good relations with Japan.

After the United States' entry in World War II against Japan, the United States, alarmed by the possibility of sabotage from Japanese-Americans along the Pacific coast and the idea that persons of Japanese ancestry were potentially disloyal, President Franklin D. Roosevelt issued Order No. 9066 on February 19, 1942. At that time, about 40,869 Japanese aliens and 76,484 Nisei or American-born Japanese living in California, Oregon, and Washington were put in relocation camps in Arkansas, Colorado, Utah, and other states. Untold hardships were suffered by the Japanese. Almost overnight they were forced to sell their property, surrender their jobs and move to a new location. Many kept their possessions in California by renting their homes or leasing their businesses. They had to re-establish themselves in a community far from their native California homes.

"The Supreme Court ruled that after the loyalty of these people was established restrictions that were not legally imposed upon all other persons could not be placed on their freedom to travel." [24]

Japanese have been refused services in beauty shops, barbershops, hotels and restaurants run by Caucasians. The Japanese, therefore, have been forced to develop their own communities. These "island communities" are found in many cities and adhere strongly to ancestral beliefs, practices, and language.

It was a misfortune that the Chinese arrived in America at the time the country's attention was focused on the question of slavery. Americans started to deal with the Chinese with nondiscriminating measures but found it in conflict with Negro and Indian policies.

Persecution of Chinese began in the early 1850's when white laborers found themselves unable to compete with the more industrious Chinese. Often a newspaper mentioned the murder of a Chinese, seldom were the murderers hanged. In several parts of California, houses of Chinese were destroyed and the Chinese were driven away from their place of occupation. Those who employed them occasionally suffered cruel beatings, even death, at the hands of hoodlums.

During 1860, thousands of Chinese coolies were imported to build railroads. The Chinese remained to work on farms or become house servants, laundrymen or merchants. The Chinese employees were desirably cheap, submissive, and efficient sources of labor. The depression of California in the 1870's

---

[24] James MacGregor Burns and Jack Walter Peltason, *Government by the People* (Englewood Cliffs, N. J.: Prentice Hall, Inc., 1960), p. 228.

was blamed on the Chinese. Mobs fought them; killing and burning the homes of others.

The Chinese at first had been looked upon as a god-send, but difference in color, dress, manner, and religion became a source of conflict. The behavior of the Chinese aroused both curiosity and suspicion. Early immigrants were uneducated, unfamiliar with customs and culture of their new land. They understood little English, did their hair in queues, lived in seclusion, and ate strange food. Some people felt the standard of living of the Chinese prevented them from becoming a part of American life. Chinese were denied the right of naturalization, had no vote, and politicians crusaded against them without much opposition. For a number of years, Chinese could not obtain permission to bring their wives to this country. They also always had trouble bringing their children. The Chinese Exclusion Act of 1882 prohibited the immigration of Chinese laborers and denied American citizenship to native Chinese until World War II. In 1943, Chinese were made eligible for citizenship and given a quota of 105 immigrants per year.

Chinatown is neither American nor Chinese. The Chinese came to America for different reasons than most immigrants. They wanted to preserve their way of life until they could return in rich splendor to China.

The Chinese mining workers and other laborers belonged to no labor unions. They seldom patronized rum shops. The general feeling was the Chinese were weaklings. They denied themselves many recreations and lived frugally which caused many Caucasians to think they were men of few wants.

In 1870 a "cubic air" ordinance was passed. It required that lodging houses provide at least 500 cubic feet of clean atmosphere for each person in his or her apartment. By 1873 this remained in force only in Chinese quarters. When Chinese landlords and lodgers refused to pay fines, prisons were soon filled. Three other ordinances were passed, all aimed at Chinese. The "queue ordinance," in which every male imprisoned in the county jail was required to have his hair cut by clippers to a uniform length of one inch from the scalp, is one of these.

The California school law in 1870, separated schools for whites and other races. It was amended in 1880 to provide segregated education for Chinese children.

The color barrier is the main stumbling block in the lives of American-born Chinese. Intermarriage between Chinese and whites has not been frequent, since it is not favored among people of either race. Some states have laws forbidding such marriages.

The opposition to Chinese has been social, economic, and racist. The Chinese lived more or less isolated from the community. Because of language and customs and by their temperament they tended to segregate themselves. Religiously, they were apart. Sociologically they were strangers in a strange land. Their lower standard of living enabled them to accept lower wages, their willingness to perform any function, no matter how menial, and their unavoidable competition with American workers condemned them in powerful labor organizations. "The Chinese, with the possible exception of the technical and scientific fields, have not been granted sufficient opportunity." [25]

## CONCLUSION

To maintain dominance a majority uses three techniques against minority groups. They are restricted by various devices to lower positions in the economy; restrictive legislation is used to erect barriers against the minorities, and efforts to deny citizenship to members of minorities have been applied. In conclusion, all the above may be applied to the Negroes, American Indians, Mexicans, Japanese, and Chinese discussed in this paper.

Segregation and discrimination of Negroes rank in this order according to Arnold Rose " (1) ban on intermarriage and other sex. Relations involving white women and colored men take precedence before anything else . . . therefore follows (2)

[25] S. W. Kung, *Chinese in American Life* (Seattle: University Press, 1962), p. 177.

all sorts of taboos and etiquettes in personal contact; (3) segregation in schools and churches; (4) segregation in hotels, restaurants, theaters, and other public conveyances; (5) discrimination in public services; and finally inequality in (6) politics; (7) justice and (8) breadwinning and relief." [26] The above may well apply to other minorities discussed in this paper.

The minority has never had a chance to feel superior. He has been made to feel that he is not capable of helping others because he can have nothing worthwhile to offer.

One of the most perplexing problems of education in America today is that of providing a quality education for all children without either sacrificing the educational opportunities of the majority group or arousing the resentment of the minority group by seeming to condescend.

It is evident that minority groups have made their greatest progress since World War II. The Negroes have received the greatest attention and advanced faster, but their achievements have had an impact on the other minority groups.

The research for this paper was made before the death of Dr. Martin Luther King. What effect his assassination will have upon the continued progress of the Negro remains a question. Will peaceful means be the answer or will the militant group take over? Many people believe that the Negro wants too much too fast. The motto of those growing up in the ghetto might be, "We just want what we ain't got." This applies to all minority groups.

In conclusion it might be said . . . "For the fact remains that the whole racial intolerance has seldom destroyed the intended victim, it has almost always, in the end, destroyed the society in which it flourished. . . . For the rights of each of us in a democracy can be no stronger than the rights of our weakest minority." [27]

---

[26] Rose, p. 195.
[27] McWilliams, p .279.

# CHAPTER VI

# Advertising in America

Each day in America one can hardly turn around without seeing an advertisement which either proclaims the glory of a product or gives the public information of some kind. Billboards, neon signs, posters, magazines, car cards, just to name a few, can be seen everywhere.

A number of economic, social, and technological factors influenced the rise of advertising in the United States. The tremendous expansion in industrial facilities that occurred after the Civil War enabled many manufacturers to mass-produce goods of uniform quality for the first time. Through the great advances in transportation, these goods could be distributed quickly over wide areas. Manufacturers soon realized that by means of advertising they could reach potential customers and persuade people to buy, and there was now an abundance of machine-made goods in relation to the demand, a crucial factor in the growth of advertising. Large-scale advertising came with the emergence of large corporations. In many cases, advertising was in part a cause as well as a result of the expansion of these companies.

Technological milestones in the various communications industries have greatly affected advertising. Some key events were the invention of the rotary press in 1849, the manufacture of paper from wood pulp in 1866, the introduction of the linotype in 1884, and the half-tone engraving in 1893, and the development of radio and television in the twentieth century. During this time there was a substantial increase in national literacy, which advanced from 86.7 per cent in 1888, to 94.0 per cent in 1920, and to more than 97 per cent in the 1960's. Congress furnished a big incentive to magazines and newspapers when it passed a law establishing second-class postal rates for printed matter. It then became profitable for publishers to seek national circulations for magazines, aided by advertising.

At first, advertising technique was limited to attracting the reader's attention. Gradually what was said became more important, and copy writing was accented. Typography was improved for greater readability. Type faces were selected to match the theme of the advertisements, and illustrations were chosen for greater interest value and for association with the goods for sale. When radio came into use, new techniques adapted to the appeal of the human voice were developed. With the expansion of media and markets, the advertiser needed more facts, and market research became a part of the advertising business. Ways of linking the many different branches and media of advertising into a coordinated campaign were required, and careful planning of advertising became necessary.

In order to reach the multitudes of people in the world and to attract their attention, advertisers developed several types of advertising to put forth their ideas. One of the most used types is retail advertising. Its main objective is to bring rapid turnover of merchandise. Retailers use merchandising copy that often stresses price reduction appeal, as well as stressing the merits of products sold at regular prices. Often, retailers and manufacturers share the costs of retail promotion in what is known as cooperative advertising.

National advertising aims at creating a less immediate result than retail advertising. It creates consumer acceptance for a brand characterized by a trade-mark or some other identifiable symbol. Through this advertising, consumers receive information about nationally distributed merchandise. Another type, advertising of services, may be either retail or national, depending on the geographic area where the services are available. The fifth type, mail-order advertising, works by reaching

69

consumers in all parts of the country for immediate sale of goods shipped directly to the consumer.

Through public relations advertising, companies attempt to build product acceptance, to attract and hold stockholders, to build employee loyalty, and to ward off political attack. Another form, international advertising, has two vital functions. It must pre-sell in the absence of a widely scattered sales organization, and it must build a company image for manufacturers. The U.S. government discovered the power of government advertising during World War II, when the Advertising Council was formed as a nonprofit group to assist the government in vital home-front drives such as the sale of war bonds and WAC recruiting.

In an attempt to convey their messages, all types of advertising rely on several media. The advertiser tries to purchase space or time in the medium which reaches the maximum number of prospects for his particular product or service with the greatest effectiveness at the lowest cost. The selection of media to reach the right people at the right time is difficult because media are so diverse and specialized. The bases on which media are selected are the quantity of circulation or other indications of ability to buy; occupation, home ownership; and intensity of the reader interest in each medium.

Newspapers are the oldest advertising medium in the United States. The newspaper stimulates a high degree of reader interest every day. They are extremely valuable to advertisers whose message is local, timely, or different in different parts of the country. Nationally, advertisers have the opportunity for close tie-ins with local dealers who carry their products. The large department stores in every city rely heavily on newspapers as their chief medium, and in return, give them huge volume discounts.

Outdoor advertising consists of posters painted or pasted on panel boards located in strategic positions where many people will see them. Outdoor boards are designed so that their commercial message can be grasped readily to make a quick impression. In much the same manner, car cards capitalize on the longer periods of time spent in public conveyances. They are intended to keep the product's name and use in the mind of the prospect. Another medium, point-of-sale, includes the various signs, display cards, window display materials, booklets, and other printed matter used in retail stores or at the point where sales are made.

During the twentieth century, much use has been made of radio and television. One of the great appeals of radio for advertising is that it has an audience all day long. Television has the advantage of combining the impact of sight and sound. The combination of the moving picture and the speaking voice gives the advertiser something that is almost the equivalent of a door-to-door sales staff. Both have aided advertising as well as being aided by advertising themselves.

In the other important medium, magazines, advertisers benefit from the leisurely reading of the sales message printed on good quality paper, and often in color. The key factor is the editorial atmosphere. A magazine with a national reputation has an important influence on dealers and helps advertisers to gain and hold distribution. A significant development in magazine advertising began in 1959, when many publications instituted split-run, or regional editions for regional and national advertisers who wanted to reach prospects only in particular areas.

Through the use of these media, millions of people are exposed to the various products being advertised. Only the blind or deaf or those in a secluded world of their own can avoid daily contact not with just one, but with dozens of advertising media. The problem for advertisers is in making a selection. No company can hope to make a splash in all of them, but a variety of them put across the advertiser's idea with sufficient success and profit. Media are also advantageous to the consumer in that they provide him with information which he ordinarily might not have. All in all, media play an important role in advertising and its effect on American society.

But what is advertising exactly? How does one define it? There are probably as many definitions of advertising as there are advertisers. In general, all agree on one point. Fundamentally, advertising is a form of communication. Because advertising relies on language and pictorial illustrations in putting forth its message, it can be considered a form of communication. It is a means whereby a manufacturer creates an image of his product and its benefits before people who are prospective buyers.

In order to have true communication between two parties, the receiver must not only hear what has been said, he must also absorb the idea, and accept it as his own. The receiver will accept the idea only when the idea communicated is interesting, worthwhile, and helpful. In the same manner, advertisers must make their message interesting, worthwhile, and helpful if they are to have true communication with the buyer. What has been said to the buyer must be understandable, not in the sense that the words must be words which are in the listener's vocabulary, but in the sense that they convey to the reader that the proposition will make him better as a human being.

Being able to have good, effective communication with the public is an important objective of the advertiser. But, in meeting this objective, he must be very careful in the manner in which he puts across his message. Advertisers must be careful to present the product as it is, without overrating or making excessive claims which the product cannot fulfill. It is imperative for advertisers to adhere strictly to the truth. No matter how much advertisers wish to delude themselves, eventually, they will be confronted by the pure facts which they have distorted. They will be confronting reality, not life as they pictured it. Advertising which deludes the public, is simply flying in the face of reality.

Although human beings often tend to delude themselves, eventually they are faced with the facts, the truth. The religions and philosophies of the world have invented moral codes in order to help people cope with fact, with reality. Sooner or later, the facts will be brought forth before the public, and at that time, the advertisers' deceit will also be brought forth. Although people often do delude themselves, they do not like to be deluded by others, especially when the moral codes have been broken. Advertising which does this causes a bad relationship to be formed between advertiser and consumer. In the long run, both the advertiser and those subjected to it are harmed by it.

Advertising communicates to not just one or two people, but to masses of people throughout the world. In this respect, advertising can be considered an institution, one of the few institutions which can properly be called an instrument of social control. At the same time, it is an instrument of economic control, for when an abundance of products prevails, advertising is called upon to teach the mass society to crave these goods or regard them as necessities. Often people abuse the influence which advertising has upon the masses and use the institution for more than communicating facts or aiding the nation's economy. Unfortunately some use it to alter men's values and speed their adjustment to a potential abundance solely for the purpose of making a profit and not for the good of men or society.

The traditional institutions have tried to improve man and develop in him qualities of social value. For example, the church has sought to inculcate virtue and consideration of others. The schools have taken the task of stimulating ability and imparting skills. The system of free enterprise has stressed the importance of hard work and the sinfulness of unproductive occupations. The church and the school, in particular, have been very self-conscious about their role as guardians of the social values and have conducted themselves with a considerable degree of social responsibility.

In contrast to this, some advertisers do not seek to improve the individual or to impart qualities of social usefulness, unless conformity to material values may be so characterized. Even though advertising has as much social influence as religion and education, some advertisers have no social goals and no social responsibility for what they do through their influence.

Because of the greater amounts of money spent on advertising per year, as compared to other institutions, it clearly thrusts an immense impact upon the mass media and in turn, upon the public in general. The impact is felt through the quantity of space it occupies in the newspapers and magazines, and the amount of time it occupies in radio and television broadcasts. This is important not only because of the influence upon the media, but because of the advertising matter itself. For these reasons, it is important that advertisements reflect only the truth. Unfortunately, some advertisers do not realize this and are more interested in the monetary rewards of advertising and not in the good which it will bring to society. In their efforts to gain the monetary rewards, they will resort to many techniques of persuasion that do not always paint a true picture. Granted, advertising must paint colorful pictures in order to be interesting, but it must also paint truthful pictures to be in the public's best interest.

It is important, from a moral point of view, to note some of the actual techniques that are used in the process of persuasion. First of all, advertisers are taking advantage of the many logical fallacies possible in the limited human thinking. An unscrupulous advertiser will use all sorts of fallacious reasoning processes in an attempt to persuade the inattentive potential buyer. For example, a cigarette will simply claim to contain no more than one-fourth of one per cent nicotine, but will not mention that this is a greater quantity than that of most other cigarettes and still insufficiently low to protect health. Also, advertisers of patented food additives, deficiency correctors, and vitamin preparations are frequently shown by the Food and Drug Administration to have misrepresented their products under tags such as "works many times faster," or "contains twice as much."

Unfortunately, the buyer has no ready standard of reference by which he can determine the quality of the goods in question. The average citizen has little opportunity to acquaint himself with the real nature of the things he buys or to protect his rights to fair exchange. The buyer has no alternative but to place a great deal of confidence in the truthfulness and honesty of the merchandiser and the advertising people who represent him.

Aside from actual misrepresentation of products, the persuasive techniques of modern advertisers make use of appeals to the subconscious needs, desires and drives. Surveys show that more than two-thirds of Americ s hundred largest advertisers have geared their campaigns to the findings of depth interview and to the advice and practical philosophy of psychiatrists.[1] The factors which ad men particularly dwell on are the drive to conformity, the obsession for taste pleasures, and the yearning for security.

One of the most prominent forms of research being used to determine why consumers buy a product and, what is equally significant, why some prospects refuse to purchase a product. The use of Freudian interpretations of the unconscious to explain consumer behavior is probably the most publicized and controversial of motivational techniques. This method was attacked in Vance Packard's *The Hidden Persuaders*.[2] Mr. Packard shows how the psychologist-advertisers encouraged housewives to buy family food on the basis of nonrational and impulsive factors. He also points out how man's deepest sexual sensitivities and yearnings were delved into and exploited for commercial profit. He also states that an attitude of cheerfulness rather than of truthfulness came to be the mark of economic reports and forecasts.

To play on man's psychic weaknesses and unconscious vulnerabilities, raises a number of serious moral questions. One viewpoint is stated by Thomas P. Coffey when he declares,

> Not a single philosophical or theological principle of traditional Western thought will condone this exploitation of the human personality. . . . Exploitation there has always been; but this debasing of human society to a series of mere "technical relations" marks a new and frightening stage in Western culture.[3]

Another morally questionable technique of persuasion in modern advertising comes from its associating between "dis-

---

[1] Poyntz Tyler, *Advertising in America* (New York: The H. W. Wilson Company, 1959), p. 173.

[2] Vance Packard, *The Hidden Persuaders* (New York: David McKay Co., 1957), p. 153.

[3] Tyler, *Advertising in America* (New York: The H. W. Wilson Company, 1959), p. 174.

tinctive" and "highly appealing" personalities with products that mainly are undistinctive. Here advertising ceases to be a discussion of a product's merits and advantages.

It should be recognized that some of the advertising associations have shown themselves soberly aware of the power they wield and are desirous of using it for the public good. But it is the very nature of advertising that it must aim for a mass appeal, and it is the nature of the mass media that they must present any item whether it be an idea, fact, or point of view, in such a way that it will attract the maximum number of readers. Hence, begins the never-ending cycle. Mass appeal is necessary in order to have mass circulation and the resulting revenue from it, and advertising is essential to enable the magazine to sell at a price that will secure millions of readers. Therefore, the contents must be addressed to millions. To do this, they must suppress any controversial or esoteric aspects of the item, and express it in the simplest of terms. These terms are usually emotional rather than rational, because emotional impulses of people are more uniform than are the mental processes of individuals.

These factors of simplification, of intensifying feeling, and fixing attention of the whole audience are all related in that their main concern is finding a message that will hold an audience rather than finding an audience to hear the message. The message must not diminish the audience either by antagonizing it or leaving anyone out of it.

In order to obtain this equilibrium, there are several guidelines followed by advertising companies. For instance, a message must not deal with subjects of special or out-of-the-way interest, since these subjects do not appeal to the majority of the audience. Secondly, it must not deal with any subject at a high level of maturity, for many people are immature and would be left out. Third, it must not deal with matters which are controversial, unpleasant, or distressing, since such matters may antagonize or offend some members of the audience.

In dealing with each separately, it must be pointed out that many perfectly unoffensive and noncontroversial subjects are excluded from the media simply because these subjects ap-

76

peal only to a limited number of people. Being directed to the masses, the media must avoid consideration of subjects which interest only the hundreds or the thousands. The danger seen in this is the censorship of a great range of subjects. This suppression is imposed by public indifference or more precisely, by the belief of those who control the media that the public would be indifferent.

Closely related to the exclusion of certain subjects is the avoidance of mature treatment of subjects which are accepted. In researching, this writer found a statement pertinent to this topic stated by Paul F. Lazarsfeld, chairman of the Department of Sociology at Columbia University, who has investigated this aspect of the matter, specifically in connection with radio. Mr. Lazarsfeld states that his studies show that the new media usually create a more hazy knowledge and a less acute interest in those events that the traditional and smaller groups of people with long established new interests.[4] This seems to be partially because Americans do not study topics in depth as they once did, before the media brought out the condensed versions.

Finally, there is the avoidance of the controversial or distressing issues. This is concerned not only with matters such as labor unionization, racial relations, or the like, but more fundamentally in the creation of a stereotype society from which all questions of social importance are screened out. In a sense this could be referred to as tolerance, but it deals with ideas not by weighing them, but by diluting them. By not dealing with such subjects, society is in a sense relieving itself of the responsibility to hear them.

The only exception to this third area of concern is the realm of politics. Here antagonistic points of view do receive hearing, but it is only in this realm where the recognition of many viewpoints (actually a limited number of them) is permitted. However, in the area of politics, although many pamphlets and other political literature present both arguments,

------

[4] Paul Lazarsfeld, *The Responsibilities of American Advertising,* 1920-1940 (New Haven: Yale University Press, 1958), p. 109.

the opponents' beliefs are often twisted and parts of speeches are omitted in an attempt to distort his beliefs. In the same manner, if a candidate's views are not conducive to public opinion on a certain issue, he often resorts to overlooking the issue, mentioning it as little as possible. Because of this factor, even in the area of politics, many social questions and problems of American life are never discussed.

Although many fallacies can be seen in advertising, many extremely important and helpful aspects can also be seen. Advertising has come to play an extremely important role in the modern American society and has benefited this society in many ways. For example, advertising speeds the introduction of new products that are needed, as well as, safeguarding the position of established products for which there is still a need. New items are accepted more quickly and at least cost, through advertising. This also leaves room for the small advertiser to get started and to compete with national advertisers. As the new products come on the market, however, the advertiser of the older products must keep his market position. He must continually remind the public of the benefits of his product or others will reap the profits.

Competition between companies is facilitated through advertising. Advertising sets up a free competitive market where the public gets a full view of what the choice is—in products, trademarks, and prices. People know who is making what, how much the price is, where it is for sale, and why the manufacturer feels his product offers a bigger benefit. At the same time, advertising is protecting against destructive price competition. The majority of the time, advertising tends to reduce prices, because each manufacturer wishes to sell his wares cheaper than his competitor.

Advertising is helpful in that it protects against infringers. The fact that a trademark is advertised proves its existence and value as far as the law is concerned. One of the most helpful pieces of evidence in any court case in support of a trademark is the proof that the mark has been widely and properly advertised. Because of this, it is well known in its field.

Public interest is enhanced when advertising is used as a servant of the public. Business groups and individuals often use advertising in an effort tc further the public welfare. One example of this is the contributions of the Advertising Council in behalf of the Red Cross. Another is the campaign to stamp out forest fires. Other examples are the advertisements used to help direct rescue operations in flood and disaster areas and the campaign to "Get Out the Vote." In the area of legislation and politics, advertisement gives free expression of public opinion about the legislation and the policies of political candidates of all (both) parties. These help maintain the freedom of expression that is part of the democratic heritage.

Another role of advertising is the friendly relations it establishes between the advertiser and the public. This type of advertising is different from that which aims at selling goods. By creating a friendly atmosphere and respect for company policies, good public relations advertising contributes to greater business efficiency.

By its very nature, advertising helps stabilize a business. It builds market acceptance before the product is brought out and leads to stable operations. The advertiser is able to invest part of the proceeds of his most profitable business years in building up a heap of consumer desires that can be tapped in later years when his market may be depressed. In a similar manner, advertising is a great help to many companies in eliminating seasonal slumps.

Unlike other institutions, advertising has the power to create desire where no desire existed before. By presenting new ideas favorably, it broadens the horizons of the people who are reached by it. In doing so, advertising breeds dissatisfaction, but it is dissatisfaction of a good kind. It is the kind that tells us, "Old ways of doing things are no longer good enough for me. I want something better." In these and many other ways, advertising has served society.

What connection, if any, can be seen between advertising and education? In a sense, advertising is simply teaching people about something. The message may warn people of the dangers of forest fires, or it may tell the public Crest yields fewer cavities, but at any rate, it is giving people information. As it gives them this information, it broadens their knowledge and hopefully, helps them lead a better, more enriched life. Advertising gives them an association with ideas and products they ordinarily might never come into contact with.

Unfortunately not all advertising messages are completely truthful, and some use psychology and persuasion to distort the facts. Education can play a great role by helping the public effectively to judge the advertisements which it sees. Starting in first grade and continuing throughout school, students can be encouraged and taught to read critically, to read between the lines, and to see the hidden idea which is so often present, but overlooked. In later grades, high school in particular, some part of the curriculum should present to students, the various kinds of advertising and the many techniques and appeals which are used. The students should be shown how a message can be distorted without being untrue. Psychology courses are particularly helpful in bringing out the various forms of psychological persuasion which are sometimes employed. Not all of the time should be spent showing the defects in advertising. No curriculum should overlook its importance as a force of social change, the role it plays in the economy, and the many other valuable assets it provides. Education, in general, has two functions relating to advertisement. First, it must educate people to the fallacies which exist and in turn, which must be corrected. Secondly, it can aid the people in bettering the aspects of the institution which are already outstanding.

Advertising, *per se,* is not a new phenomenon. Its history dates back thousands of years. A century ago, however, advertising was a very minor form of economic activity. But those days are gone forever. Advertising was brought into being by existing abundances; producers recognizing the possibilities of this medium, made changes in form, in economic interests which advertised, and in the nature of appeal. Today, advertising has become an institution as powerful, if not moreso, as the church and the school. It dominates the media, has vast power in shaping popular standards, and exercises social control. It has become one of the most widely used forms of communication putting forth its message by the use of the various types of advertising in many different media.

As does every other institution which carries such power, influence, and importance, advertising has its faults. People abuse its very nature of communication and make it even more open to criticism of all sorts by all people. Even though it has faults, American society needs it. People want it and depend upon it for a great amount of information. Economically, advertising plays a great role in American society, not only by stimulating the sale of goods, but by providing the greatest amount of income of the broadcasting, newspaper, and magazine companies, and by providing many public services. In essence, advertising has become the spark plug of the American economy.

Advertising is an integral part of the American way of life. Honesty of purpose and a clear concept of duty coupled with responsible criticism and improvement, being encouraged by a well-educated public, can help advertising make creditable contributions to the well-being and happiness of the society. In doing so, it will be worthy of the power which it holds over the society.

I have tried to show here the good and the bad points of advertising, the advantages and disadvantages, it has in its present condition.

# CHAPTER VII

# Mass Communication: How It Affects American Society

The American citizen is continually bombarded by mass media and mass communication; the only time he is free from this mass media is when he is sleeping. It seems as though the only way to completely escape this bombardment is to revert to the life of the hermit. Even then, in this modern society, one might not be able to escape. After all, he might look up to the sky one day and see the Goodyear Blimp, or even an airplane towing a huge "Eat at Joe's" sign.

To understand mass media and mass communication, let me begin by giving a definition of each of these terms. "Mass communication" refers to the process of sending identical messages to large numbers of people who are physically separated and who are in different walks of life. "Mass media" refers to the instruments that make this process of mass communication possible.

Communication is the propagator of the social process. It is the means by which men exchange and transmit knowledge. It is the means by which men organize, stabilize, and modify the social life and pass on its forms and meaning from generation to generation. It is also used to standardize knowledge and provide uniformity. Today, in America, mass communication is used to regiment people and make them conform to the wishes of those who control mass communication just as, in the past, brute force was used to make people conform to the wishes of those who held the power. The role played by the mass media in the lives of the Americans can be fairly obvious if we take the time to think about it. They are entirely dependent upon the media for news and knowledge of events. Great business complexes have been established to let these people know what happens in the world. In addition to providing information, the media also provide entertainment and education. This phenomenon, mass communication, is in its infancy when compared to the age of other American institutions. Nevertheless, it is as important, if not moreso, as any other American institution.

The media can be classified into three major categories: 1. the printed form, 2. the filmed form, and 3. the electronic form. Of these three forms, only the first is older than the twentieth century. The filmed and electronic forms are products of this century. They reached a marked degree of technical perfection which makes them adequate for mass consumption sometime between the 1920's and the 1940's.[1]

The printed form contains books, newspapers, magazines and any other printed material designed to reach a large audience. Printed material can be referred to again and again by the reader and it requires more effort on the part of the reader for its assimilation than does material presented in the other two forms.

The filmed form includes motion pictures of all varieties ranging from the multi-million dollar extravaganza to the shorts and other less expensive films.

In the electronic form, radio, television, and popular recordings are included. The electronic form is the newest and often the most controversial. Television specifically is subjected to constant criticism and will be discussed later in this chapter.

From simple to complex, any communication situation is composed of three elements: 1. a sender who wishes to communicate, 2. a message the sender wishes to convey, and 3. a receiver who wishes to receive the message. Remove any one

---

[1] Robert C. O'Hara, *Media for the Millions* (New York: Random House, 1961).

of these and there would not be a communication situation.[2] The process of mass communication, however, can exist as a situation without the receiver wishing to receive the message. This is the case with many television commercials, where the commercial conveys a message to the receiver while the receiver, in many cases, does not wish to listen.

I mentioned earlier the word "bombarded" when I referred to the overwhelming amount of mass media saturation in the United States. I came across an entire eight page chapter while doing this research. The pages of that chapter contained statistics which were amazing to me. To summarize briefly: radios are found in 97% of American homes; television sets in 86%. Daily newspapers print 58,000,000 copies each day and weekly newspapers print an additional 49,000,000 weekly. There are 8,000 periodicals published in the United States with a total publication of over 400,000,000 copies per issue, which is double the population of the United States. There are 3,526 AM radio stations, 823 FM stations and 522 television stations. Receiver sets for the total sender stations above is over 212,000,000.[3]

With this astounding number of mass media available to the American people, the Americans should be the most well-informed people in the world! As it turns out, they are as opinionated and ill-informed as any other people, if not moreso. Today, Americans live in an "age of conformity." Most of them desire to be "nice guys." Though the act of conforming is positive, many of the Americans are not positive.[4] They follow the dictates of the party line.[5] When men blindly conform in taste, belief, or action only because it is easier, they give up their birthright as individuals.[6]

This age of conformity is the most favorable atmosphere

---

[2] *Ibid.*

[3] *Ibid.*

[4] Brian McCarthy, "Age of Conformity," *Commonweal*, LXVI (June 19, 1957), p. 402.

[5] D. K. Winebrenner, "Keeping in Line," *School Arts*, LIX (December, 1959), p. 48.

[6] William H. Lowe, Jr., "The Decision to Differ," *House and Garden*, CXI (April, 1957), p. 79.

for "mass movements," because many of the people are sick of being conformists but they feel they have no other choice. The "Beat Generation" is one reply for such conformity. Peace demonstrations is another reply to it. Violent demonstration may very well be another answer to it.

The ability of mass communication media in conforming people can be observed in many different ways. One of the most easily recognized influences is advertising. Advertising not only offers products for sale, but also creates an interest for larger consumption. People are encouraged to buy a new product simply because it is stylish or "in." It makes no difference whether the product is particularly needed or not. In this way people are persuaded to conform in the type of clothing they wear, in the type of personal care items they use, and even in the type of foods they eat.[7]

Political leaders make use of mass media to express their views and hopefully to conform the public to their ideas.[8] They fully realize that their political future depends on the uniformity of the people.[9] They reach voters through radio interviews, television panel discussions, and newspaper and magazine articles. The politician is judged considerably on his personality. Television can emphasize or minimize certain personal characteristics. Some political figures have benefited from television campaigning while others have suffered greatly from it. The improvement of recording devices permits the speaker to talk in his natural tone of voice. The naturalness of voice, along with the image of the speaker, makes the television contact between the candidate and the voters seem personal and direct.[10]

The public uses mass communication media as a source of control over government officials: "The news media have also the vital role of 'watchdog' over the government, searched out

[7] Educational Policies Commission, p. 33.

[8] Edwin Emery, Philip H. Ault, and Warren K. Agee, *Introduction to Mass Communications*, p. 15.

[9] Educational Policies Commission, p. 36.

[10] Amy Loveman, "Weapons of Will," *Saturday Review*, XXXV (November 29, 1952), p. 22.

instances of malfunctioning and corruption." [11] In this way it can make the officials "conform" to the constitutional laws in order to be re-elected.

It seems that the appearance of someone or something in print, or on the air or film gives it stature. People are greatly influenced by the personalities so presented. This fact is very well illustrated by the following quote:

> Not only may wants and needs, in the material sense, tend toward uniformity under the impact of the media of mass communication; so may behavior. The model of speech presented by radio and television, for example, has had much to do with the decline of regional accents in American speech and the growth of what language scholars call "standard American." [12]

Personalities often introduce fads in dress or hair styles. There have even been several instances that entertainers were elected to political offices. Such influences were not known before mass communication media. [13]

International propaganda has been greatly expanded through the use of mass communication media. The United States has been the target for extensive propaganda campaigns. People in other countries have been made to conform in their distrust and dislike for all Americans. Americans are unused to this and usually feel angered, hurt, and bewildered. Even some of the United States' proudest institutions are attacked by propaganda. [14]

Mass communication media in itself encourages conformity in that it treats the public as one big majority. All peoples are given what the majority wants. Frank Luther Mott states this well: "It is as though the media were saying to us: 'You are all modern Americans; therefore, you must all have the same interests, tastes, intelligence, and desires.' " [15] Part of this

---

[11] Emery, Ault, and Agee, p. 17.
[12] Educational Policies Commission, p. 35.
[13] *Ibid.*, p. 340-43.
[14] *Ibid.*, p. 40-43.
[15] Mott, p. 60.

fault lies in the fact that the media have to serve people of different locations and social and economical backgrounds.

Mass communication media can influence people to conform in useful ways also. Three examples are: the influence to campaign against a dreaded disease, the campaign to reduce traffic accidents, and the campaign to vote.[16]

"Has human society become a kind of puppet at the end of a string called 'communication,' responsive to tugs in the hands of experts?"[17] I am afraid this is the case for most of the Americans. Most of them are content to read the newspaper, mainly the comic section, and listen to a fifteen-minute news report on television to gain their insight in world affairs. So, all that the experts have to do is pull these strings in the direction to make people believe only what the experts want them to believe. I am not saying that every television or newspaper report is a lie, but I am saying that the Americans do not hear the truth in all cases. For propaganda to be effective the target should be the committed as well as the uncommitted peoples. Although propaganda exchanges seldom convince the already committed. The "battle for men's minds" is mainly a struggle for the minds of these uncommitted and restless people, the "silent majority."

My conclusion on this point of propaganda is that the audience is generally more receptive when the media communicate life mainly in emotional terms rather than in rational or logical terms. In this way the media can appeal to a large number of people on common grounds.

How does mass communication effect education? I define education as the process of growing up mentally, physically, and socially. It is the art of bringing up a child to live the "good life" in a particular society.

In today's society the students' horizons are vastly enlarged due to mass communication. The school age child of 1900 never heard another language spoken, unless he lived in an area where immigrants concentrated, he had no mental picture of a joint session of Congress. He never saw a baseball game, an

---

16 Educational Policies Commission, p. 33.
17 *Ibid.,* p. 32.

opera, a Presidential inauguration, the Kentucky Derby, or the British Ambassador. Today all these things are routine to adults and students alike. The American student, because of this nation's development of mass communication, has the raw material of knowledge in his hands to an extent unknown at the turn of the century. He is thus much more informed than was his grandfather; however, my feeling on this matter is that this new knowledge, vicariously and easily arrived at, is not necessarily profound, meaningful, or even accurate.

Mass communication increases the commonness of experience among students. Today's classroom teacher frequently has the experience of discovering that most students present have seen the same movie or television program or, more rarely, read the same book.

Mass communication also creates a strong pressure to conform. Although the difference in degree and direction might have to go unmeasured, two things could be concluded: 1. the human tendency to be transformed and made to conform is very strong, 2. modern mass communication has turned this tendency into a living practice, more widespread than was likely to exist before.

The formal process of education will continue to add new things, but it has the additional obligation of bringing order and perspective and selectivity to what is already present as well as to help the individual screen the constant flood of new stimuli which will pour in from communication.

It is the belief of some that through mass communication information and ideas are circulated to the population at large, and in turn reflect the opinions and attitudes of public and organized groups within the public. In America the newspapers, radio, and magazine decide what to report back. The media's freedom in choosing whom to write about and whom to focus the camera on and whom to quote, determines what the American people know and talk about. In sum, they have been "swallowed up in mass media." [18] As for its future poten-

---

[18] Herbert Brucker, "Mass Man and Mass Media," *Saturday Review*, XLVIII (May 29, 1965), p. 14.

tial, mass communication through the mass media can break the bonds of distance and isolation and can be a very useful factor in social, national, and international development.

# CHAPTER VIII

# The Americans' Lack of Knowledge of Other Countries

The people of the United States have, in general, little knowledge about the other countries of the world. This lack of knowledge is evident in almost every phase of American life and causes many problems both within the country and outside it in terms of foreign relations. There is no easy remedy for this problem, but there are certain programs and changes that can and should be instigated in the United States and all over the world.

First of all, I must define the term "knowledge" as used in this writing. By "knowledge of other countries," I mean factual knowledge and understanding of the habits, customs, religions, governments, and economic structures of other countries. This knowledge connotes acceptance of other cultures—not necessarily as being "good" (moral judgment) —but as being serviceable and convenient for those particular countries. By "lack of of knowledge," I mean not only a complete absence of knowledge, but also incomplete, false, or twisted facts which are substituted for knowledge. Also, I mean lack of knowledge not only of the smaller countries but also of the larger countries such as, England, France, China, Russia.

A great part of the information which Americans have about other countries is stereotype or generalization. They "know" that Scottish people are stingy, Frenchmen are temperamental, Germans are gruff, Africans are primitive, Orientals are silent but wily, Arabs are camel-drivers, and so on.

Many people are content with this type of knowledge and make no attempt to seek more information or even to seek proof of what they have heard. Complete belief in these types of information has diminished, but their repercussions can still be seen in the lives of many Americans. The extent to which the prejudice based on stereotypes is handed down from generation to generation is the extent to which these types of beliefs continue to harm the United States.

In U.S. homes, schools, and businesses, people are obviously centered completely around the "American" ways of doing things. It is a rare and special occasion when a housewife incorporates into her daily schedule a custom of a foreign country. They presume, simply because a custom or habit is native to the United States, that that habit is best. How many Americans regularly make authentic foreign dishes, experiment with foreign fashions and furnitures, or take a genuine interest in studying other languages, governmental systems, or philosophies? The key word here is "genuine." Many people, for social prestige, flaunt superficial interest and "knowledge" of other countries. This interest—not being genuine—shows no regard for the countries themselves.

When one considers all of the information which can and should be known about the world's countries, one wonders how any teachers are ever considered "qualified" to teach history (even American history). Most history teachers have learned what they know simply by reading textbooks and memorizing facts. They have no first-hand knowledge of other countries. They have never lived in these countries, worshipped in their churches, shopped in their stores, attended their schools. How many of these teachers have a "genuine" interest, and how many simply need a major and choose history, and need a job and choose teaching? Not only teachers of history are involved in this lack of knowledge. English teachers are hardly qualified to instruct classes in foreign literature without knowledge of the countries from which the writings come. The same can be said of teachers of sociology, art, and music. The fields of anthropology, archeology, and geology have more factual knowledge about the countries about which they teach than the above-mentioned fields. Since education is the only means by which children and young people can learn about other countries, and education, at the present time to the average, means knowing enough to get by on the test, Americans have little chance of gleaning real "knowledge."

The United States government exhibits, almost daily, a pitiable lack of knowledge about the countries with which it deals. This lack of knowledge is caused most often by the smugness and conceit of the United States. The United States, for instance, sends tractors and often cultivating equipment—along with a few "instructors"—to teach an "underprivileged" country how to farm. These instructors perhaps have studied textbooks about the country, but they really have little valuable knowledge of the customs, likes and dislikes, and superstitions of the people with whom they are working. In the case of American aid to one country, the United States exhibited another type of stupidity. The United States shipped a huge load of farm equipment to that country, but, once it arrived there, five thousand dollars had to be paid to gangsters of that country to protect the shipment from the Communists. One would think that, before spending so much money to ship and protect these materials, the United States would investigate the situation in that country. Time and again, the United States government decides to send "help" to other countries and—because of lack of knowledge of the countries' cultures—literally has to force this "help" down the throats of the people. The so-called "experts" that the United States sends abroad are hardly what I would term real experts, considering my definition of knowledge. These experts, too often concerned with material gain, political advancement, and other goals unrelated to their jobs, may have some factual knowledge, but little true empathy with the country or its people.

The American government exhibits not only a lack of knowledge, but also a lack of respect for and lack of understanding of other countries. The words "communism" and "socialism" evoke immediately an attitude of fear and a judgment of "bad" from almost all Americans. The fact that the communistic countries of the world today do have their unique attributes and do serve certain functions is ignored in light of the fact that their systems are different from "ours."

Many social and political problems arise from the Americans' lack of knowledge of other countries. One of the more obvious problems is the difficulty they have in completely accepting into their society people from other countries, especially if those people are readily distinguished by color or other physical characteristics. This is not as great a problem as it has been in the past, but even now misunderstanding as well as prejudice make it difficult for an immigrant to be totally accepted as he is. The more quickly he adopts the American customs and ideas, however, the more quickly he will be accepted. This problem, again, stems from the Americans' lack of knowledge about the countries from which these people have come. They should not be forced into changing all of their customs; instead, the Americans should learn about, and, in turn, accept them as they are.

The United States government, which seems so concerned with its appearance in the eyes of the rest of the world, oftentimes does more harm than good to its "public image" because it does not know enough about the rest of the world. The United States, when it makes proposals to or agreements with other countries, seldom seems to be willing to meet these countries on equal bases. Instead, it assumes that the other countries (especially the smaller ones) should and will forsake their ways in favor of the American way. Because the Americans do not know enough about the cultures of these countries, they naively assume that those countries have no culture. By being pushy and showing its ignorance, the United States makes little headway in its foreign realations. It also seems that the United States not only shows its ignorance, but it assumes ignorance on the part of other countries. Within America, there is discrimination against minority groups, and cheating in and against the government. Preaching about individualism and freedom and then interfering with the individualism and freedom of other countries demonstrates again American hypocrisy. The United States has been called "the land of opportunity," the country where one can make his own choices.

But how free are Americans in making their choices when they do not have sufficient knowledge, in many cases, to make an intelligent choice?

A great social problem in the world is, and it always has been, war. In my opinion, one of the main causes for war is lack of knowledge about the people with whom one country is having difficulty. Oftentimes misconceptions arise—from lies, rumors, propaganda, etc., which circulate throughout the United States—and most citizens of this country haven't enough knowledge about the country in question to sift the facts from the lies. Malicious rumors about another country serve to build up the American ego, and sooner or later some group of United States "hawks" is ready to start a war against the country. The general public, after enough stirring speeches on "the defense of American ideals," will join the hawks' bandwagon, seldom realizing or caring that they do not know enough about the situation even to state an opinion. One wonders what these people learned in school, let alone in church or at home.

The American people are so pathetically unaware of so many things, that it is high time steps were taken to erase this apathy and naivete. The key word in this change is "reeducation"—not only of young people, but also of teachers, civic groups, tourists, and the public in general. First of all, the number and variety of courses offered in all schools—especially in elementary and secondary schools—should be increased. Elementary schools should offer solid foundations in philosophy, comparative religion, social problems, and foreign languages. In the "traditional" method of teaching, there still seems to exist a feeling that elementary school children should and can grasp only reading, writing, simple mathematics, geography, etc. But why are these children's minds so limited? They should be introduced, in a manner which they can understand, to many more of the concepts and problems with which they will be faced during their adult lives. Individual creativity in these and other areas should be stressed by means of projects, reports, discussions, and guest speakers. If a child's interest is stimulated, at an early age, the chances are good that —with continued encouragement—his zeal for knowledge will

94

not abate. Therefore, his later life will be much different from the lives of most American citizens today. With a good background in and a broad body of knowledge about many areas, he will be better equipped to make decisions. Having been brought up to think of knowledge as a wonderful thing, he will continue to seek facts and explanations, rather than to accept blindly any information that falls upon his ears. He will be not only more knowledgeable, but also interested in seeking more and more knowledge.

People who have been educated in the above manner would be much more qualified to be called "teachers" than most so-called teachers of today. But, until the time comes when we could have such teachers, we would need to gradually reeducate the instructors we have now. At first glance, this would appear to be an impossible task, but I feel that the job could be accomplished, through seminars, travel-study programs, and courses in philosophies, religions, psychology, and intellectual history. Younger teachers could probably adapt themselves more easily to a program such as this, but I think that older people, too, once they understood the purpose, could make the needed adjustments.

American tourists often cause damage to the reputation of the United States, because they flaunt abroad their lack of knowledge about the rest of the world. In my proposed re-education program, they, too, would receive countless benefits. No longer would they go into other countries showing their ignorance of foreign customs, beliefs, and governments. In their travels, they would be able to gain even more real knowledge, having had their eyes and minds opened to the "facts of life," so to speak. These people would be good ambassadors for the United States, because they could teach other countries about the United States and demonstrate that Americans are genuinely interested in them. Civic groups could also aid in the reconstruction program. They could discuss and distribute information about community life, local governments, leisure and recreation programs, etc., in towns and cities all over the world.

I feel that the attitudes of and the relations between people would change greatly if steps were taken to erase the lack of knowledge about other countries. People would have more respect for each other, and, therefore, they could get along better. Perhaps then the people of the United States could forget about national prestige and personal profit and could concentrate on seeking the truth and a peaceful world community.

# CHAPTER IX

# Freedom and Alienation in American Society

As of late, there is much written about anxiety and alienation in America, about the frustration and meaninglessness that many Americans encounter and live with. Why are such phenomena present in a society that is democratic and free? A society where even the government is one of the people, by the people and for the people? This, I think, would happen in such a society when freedom is accepted as whatever is given by one group to another, or, when it is considered to be a commodity that could be bought by money. As I look closely at those Americans who feel alienated, I find this to be the case. They feel that they are not "given" enough freedom. They think, and they have enough reason to think so, that freedom is "given" to those who have it. If they were to examine their lives, they would find out that whatever freedom they already have was given to them, but they forget the fact that they had to at least ask for it or request it, if not fight for it. Anyway, they do forget how they attain the freedom that they possess.

Freedom is not something given by one group to another; nor is it a commodity that can be purchased. It is an inalienable and inherent part of the psychic make-up of every human being. It is realized only by resisting the imposition of untenable restrictions on the exercise of a right that is already possessed by those who try to impose the restrictions, whether through law or through physical force.

97

The amazing thing is that, in this society where much is written on freedom, very few Americans know what freedom means.

"Modern European and American history is centered around the efforts to gain freedom from the political, economic, and spiritual shackles that have bound men." [1] Assuming this to be true, we can say that this has also blinded the Westerner in general, and the American in particular, to the other aspect of freedom: the freedom to. The idea of freedom has two aspects: freedom from and freedom to. Furthermore, it is impossible without restraint; "every kind of freedom involves restraint." [2]

Freedom in America is more and more related to cooperative participation. This is evident from the number of associations and organizations that exist in America. The Americans have learned that they cannot obtain freedom from want or freedom from fear without such cooperation. "The only way to maintain such freedom is by cooperating with others, not by dominating others or by submitting to their domination." [3] But this high degree of cooperation brought about some bad consequences. For one thing it brought about vagueness and ambiguity to the idea of freedom. In the American society with "a political and social environment where the spirit of freedom has been substantially developed, the commonplace individual generally has only a vague notion of the relationship that freedom bears to his personal existence. . . . To these people, the legal right to work and to travel where they elect, to vote for whom they admire, and to worship at the church of their choice constitute the whole and complete idea of freedom." [4]

Most of them forget that the problem of freedom is not

---

[1] Erich Fromm, *Escape from Freedom* (New York: Rinehart & Co., Inc., 1941), p. 3.

[2] Alan F. Griffin, *Freedom American Style* (New York: Holt & Co., 1940), p. 12.

[3] Marshall Field, *Freedom in More than a Word* (Chicago: University of Chicago Press, 1945), p. 4.

[4] Edward C. Kraus, *Origins of Conflict* (New York, Vantage Press, 1964), p. 41.

simply to preserve and increase the traditional freedom, but that it is also to gain a new kind of freedom, one which enables them to realize their own individual selves, to have faith in each individual self and in life.[5] Today, more than ever before, the serious threat to democracy is the existence within the personal attitudes and institutions of Americans of conditions which have given victory to external authority, discipline, uniformity and dependence upon a leader, and made the resort to violence a living reality in the American society.

> Capitalism not only freed man from traditional bonds, but it also contributed tremendously to the increasing of positive freedom, to the growth of an active, critical, responsible self. . . . At the same time, it has made the individual more alone and isolated and imbued him with a feeling of insignificance and powerlessness.[6]

". . . The structure of modern society affects man in two ways simultaneously: he becomes more independent, self-reliant, and critical, and he becomes more isolated, alone, and afraid." [7] "Is there a state of positive freedom in which the individual exists as an independent self and yet is not isolated but united with the world, with other men, and nature? We believe . . . that man can be free and yet not alone . . . independent and yet an integral part of mankind. This freedom man can attain by the realization of his self, by being himself." [8]

This increasingly mechanized, atomized, and depersonalized world of the Americans is rendering many an American alienated from nature, from God, and from society. The individual American is unable to achieve an identity and a relatedness to others.

> He has become estranged from himself. He does not experience himself as the center of his world, as the creator

---

[5] Fromm, p. 105.
[6] *Ibid.*, pp. 107-08.
[7] *Ibid.*, p. 104.
[8] *Ibid.*, p. 257.

of his own acts—but his acts and their consequences have become his masters, whom he obeys, or whom he may even worship. The alienated person is out of touch with himself as he is out of touch with any other person.[9]

This development of alienation in American society, though attributed to capitalism in general, is associated with a number of current social changes. I have mentioned many of these social changes in the chapter on "The Socialization of the Individual." The process of urbanization has forced millions of people to live together who do not necessarily share common values and habits of living. A part of the alienation experienced by urbanites is their inability to find a satisfying culture in the city. Alienated, they are thus capable of seeing murders committed in the streets without bothering to report them to the authorities. The following report shows how great public apathy is:

### REPORTERS STAGE FAKE CRIMES, PROVE PUBLIC APATHY IS GREAT

MIAMI, Nov. 25 (UPI)—The handcuffed man boarded a city bus in front of the jail, struggled to put his coin in the till and took a seat next to another passenger. Several blocks later, he got off the bus with no one trying to stop him.

The driver and nearly two dozen passengers who ignored the handcuffed man are called "partners in crime" in an hour-long documentary scheduled Sunday by television station WCKT.

Asked by reporters whether he noticed anything unusual about the passenger who boarded the bus in front of the jail, the driver said: "Sure, he had on handcuffs."

### LOOKED FOR POLICEMAN

The driver was asked why he didn't attempt to stop the man, and he replied: "I was going to stop him if I had seen a cop."

[9] Eric and Mary Josephson (eds.), *Man Alone—Alienation in Modern Society* (New York: Dell Publishing Co., 1962), p. 55.

Station reporters then questioned the woman who sat next to the handcuffed man and obligingly pulled the stop cord when he explained, "I can't because I'm handcuffed."

"It's none of my business," she said. "He wasn't bothering me."

This was one of the more dramatic of over 15 crimes staged by reporters with the co-operation and help of police in Miami and nearby municipalities and filmed by hidden cameras.

Also filmed were purse snatchings, shoplifting, an officer being attacked by a suspect, a child kidnapping, and a jewelry store robbery.

In only four incidents—a purse snatching, the jewelry store robbery, a shoplifting and the attack on the officer—did any of at least a half-dozen witnesses make an active attempt to stop the criminal. Two of the good Samaritans were teen-age grocery bagboys, one was a young carpenter, and the other was a Cuban woman.

### WITNESSES QUESTIONED

After each incident, witnesses were questioned and asked why they did not attempt to stop the crime, or report it to police. The most common answer:

"I didn't want to get involved . . . I was afraid . . . I thought someone else would."

News director Gene Strull said WCKT filmed the documentary to see whether there was any truth to the often-repeated complaint that people are apathetic toward crime.

"The bitter truth is that most people are apathetic," Strull said. "Frankly, I didn't think it would be as bad as it was."

The documentary points also up two common police complaints—that eyewitnesses are unreliable, and that people will let almost anyone into their homes without questioning them.

In one sequence, reporter Mike Silver ran up to a jewelry store on a busy Coral Gables street, smashed the window, scooped up a handful of merchandise and fled. No one attempted to stop Silver, who cut his arm reaching through the broken window.

101

A few minutes later, Silver returned to the scene. He had changed his shirt, but not his blood-spattered trousers. He questioned one witness, who said he could identify the burglar, for several minutes and was not recognized.

When this same incident was staged again several days later, a young carpenter who was working nearly a block away from the jewelry store took off in pursuit of Silver with a claw hammer and was about to catch him when police stepped in.

In another episode, Silver's 10-year-old daughter— screaming for help and kicking—was dragged into a car from a sidewalk in front of a shopping center dime store. Again, no one attempted to stop the "kidnappers" or reported the incident to police.

One truck driver who witnessed the "kidnapping from inside a snack shop 20 feet away was asked what he did. "I just kept eating," he said.

## GIFT OFFERED

Steve Greenwald, associate producer of the documentary, then picked up the telephone and called 12 housewives, offering them a gift for trying a new laundry soap. He asked them when they would be away from home so he would not deliver their gift at the wrong time.

Six of the women gave Greenwald specific times when they would not be home. Police said this was a common trick used by burglars to find out when houses they intend to rob would be unoccupied.

In still another episode, an off-duty policeman was dressed in civilian clothes, given a battery charger and an obviously phony identification card and sent door-to-door to "check for radiation in your television set."

He went to 12 homes and was admitted without trouble to 13. The neighbor of one home the television tester checked insisted that his set be checked also.[10]

---

[10] "Reporters Stage Fake Crimes, Prove Apathy Is Great," *St. Louis Post-Dispatch*, Sunday, November 26, 1967, sec. A, p. 26.

Industrialization has contributed its share to the alienation of the workers—they no longer make products; they make parts. They are being denied creativeness, curiosity, and independent thought. Manager and owner are alienated as well.

The process of consumption is as alienating as the process of production. Americans acquire things by money, they are accustomed to it and take it for granted but actually, this is a most peculiar way of acquiring things. Such an act of consumption is essentially a satisfaction of artificially stimulated fantasies, a performance alienated from a concrete, real self.

The alienated attitude toward consumption is more apparent in the consumption of activities used to substitute for leisure. Here in this area, the American is most passive and alienated. He "consumes" ball games, moving pictures, newspapers and magazines, books, lectures, "social" gatherings, in the same way in which he consumes the commodities he has bought. I sometimes wonder how they can possibly enjoy entertainment, especially professional sports, when it is bought in the same manner as a pair of shoes is bought. I also wonder who or which is consumed, the ball game or the spectator!

The American, nowadays, experiences himself as a thing to be employed successfully on the market. A thing to be bought just as he himself buys what he consumes. He rarely experiences himself as the bearer of human powers. He is alienated from these powers. If you ask an American, "What are you?" he answers, "I am a student," "I am a salesman," "I am a doctor," etc. This alienated personality which is for sale, at a price, loses a good deal of the human dignity which is so characteristic of man even in the most primitive cultures. There is aloneness and alienation in the Americans' failure to enjoy the deep and personal contacts they dream of having. People may be married for many years, yet, despite the fact that they continue to live together, feel a void rather than a closeness in their relationship. The absence of strong family ties is a kind of aloneness too; it contributes its share to alienation. Yet, the psychologists and sociologists still maintain, man is a social being with a deep need to share, to help, to feel as a member of a group.[11]

---

[11] Josephson, p. 69.

How could this alienated person be healthy? He experiences himself as a thing, an investment to be manipulated by himself and by others; thus he becomes lacking in a sense of self. This lack of self creates deep anxiety. It is primarily because of this anxiety, generated by the lack of self, that the modern age has been called "the age of anxiety." [12]

Every alert citizen of the American society realizes, on the basis of his own experience as well as his observation of his fellowmen, that anxiety is a pervasive and profound phenomenon in the middle of the twentieth century. He would be aware not only of the more obvious anxiety-creating situations in our day, such as threats of war, of the uncontrolled atom bomb, and the radical political and economic upheaval but also of less obvious, deeper, and more personal sources of anxiety in himself as well as in his fellow-men—namely, the inner confusion, psychological disorientation, and uncertainty with respect to values and acceptable standards of conflict.[13]

The pressure toward conformity, the fear of disapproval, and competition are other sources of anxiety and guilt feeling. Anxiety, guilt feelings, and alienation lead to the loss of the individual's true self—his self as he truly is—and opens the door to more hypocrisy and more guilt feelings and more alienation. Something must be done, and very soon to restore the warm, personal relationships that are necessary for a healthy, human life.

[12] Erich Fromm, *The Sane Society* (New York: Rinehart, 1955), p. 204.

[13] Maurice R. Stein, *et al.* (ed.), *Identity and Anxiety* (Illinois: The Free Press of Glencoe, 1960), p. 120.

# CHAPTER X

# The Sexual Revolution within the American Society: Individual Relationship to Family and Community

Today in America we find an ingredient of concern voiced in writings, lectures, and through means of mass media by individuals interested in the morals of the country.

This concern revolves around a current concept in the American society which has been popularly called the "Sexual Revolution." So much has been written on this subject by many well-meaning, but sometimes confused persons that readers of the literature on the subject feel lost in the array of conflicting views and ideas presented. Many professional organizations, individuals, and professional men contribute to the mass of materials available on the subjects of family relations, sex education, family life, and child development. This fact alone explains why there is so much controversy regarding the topic.

To be sure, there is a change occurring in the sexual mores of Americans; however, the major problems are to understand what these changes are, what is causing them, and what implications they have for the young adults: the prospective teachers, parents, and members of the community.

The most appropriate place to begin is to discuss the forces present in the American society which are causing these changes in the sexual mores to occur. These forces may include such things as the population explosion, the scientific advances, the wars, cultural interchanges, communication media, and other factors.

The inhabitants of America are able to move from place to place with little or no difficulty. This fact has a pronounced effect on the sexual mores of these people. The Americans are no longer isolated on farms or in rural settings. This change from a predominantly rural population to a highly urbanized one was a major factor in this and other changes in American social behavior. Urban life offers much greater competition. The demands for better housing, clothes, jobs, and more freedom conflicts with the desire for more children. Birth control practices have been adopted in many instances because of wanting to advance oneself. Old forms of social control break down in such a setting, and along with this idea comes the new concept regarding the sexual act. This is also enhanced because, in all states, contraceptives are sold and used, and because courts have generally upheld the usage of these devices as legal. The Federal government has upheld the use of contraceptives also and has aided many organizations in this country and abroad to set up family planning programs to enable individual families to have the number of children they want at the time sequence they want to have them. Consequently, people are forced to re-evaluate their sexual mores.

As the extended kinship system dissolves or loses its importance, mate selection processes become a more personal responsibility, and the importance of peer group norms increases and takes precedence over family norms.[1]

Today people in the United States are so mobile, they do not stay in one area for any great length of time. This can result in social rebuttal, sexual deviations, and promiscuity. People can engage more freely in practices or beliefs regarding their sex roles.

It is also logical to assume that when a country has a highly mobile population, it will also necessarily have a high degree of cultural interchange. The influence of this cultural inter-

---

[1] Rita Seiden and Edwin Smigel, *The Decline and Fall of the Double Standard* (New York: 1968), quoted in *The Annals of the American Academy of Political & Social Sciences,* Sept. 1968, p. 9.

change on the social mores of the Americans has been pronounced.

The sexual mores of the Americans are different from those of other peoples. They are even different from one religious group to another and from one coast to another as well. Because of the interchanging of ideas and beliefs of various cultures within the United States, Americans are constantly exposed to new experiences and new learning. This exposure results in a reassessment of personal values regarding sex and often an adoption of different beliefs and practices.

World War I may have had a profound impact, though not immediate or abrupt, on sexual behavior. In any war, the mores governing family life tend to decay. Removed from some of the responsibilities, restrictions, and supports of the family, removed from the all-seeing eye of the small town or neighborhood, soldiers are suddenly subject only to the most approving observations of their fellow soldiers. In the face of death or the possibility of being severely wounded, hedonism becomes the prevailing attitude. This attitude appears to be contagious and spreads to the civilian population. In World War I, this particularly affected the young women who were working in factories, taking on roles that had once belonged exclusively to men, often, for the first time, living alone in relative anonymity, and in many instances emotionally involved with men who were scheduled to be sent overseas. This same hedonistic philosophy may be held by contemporary young people who are faced with the dangers of limited wars and with the ever-present possibility of extinction by nuclear explosion. Many soldiers had contact with prostitutes and contracted venereal diseases. Venereal disease and the prostitutes taught the soldier more about sex in his relatively short career in the armed services than he might normally have learned.[2]

The soldier who went abroad had new sexual experiences and came in contact with women whose behavior derived from different and more permissible sex norms; the returned veteran

---

[2] Seiden and Smigel, *The Decline and Fall of the Double Standard* (New York: 1968, quoted in *The Annals of the American Academy of Political & Social Sciences*, Sept. 1968, pp. 9-10.

brought back with him sexual attitudes shaped by these new norms. Although they were not consciously intended for his mother, sister, wife, or wife-to-be, they tended to affect them as well.

War also tends to spread industrialization and to extend the need for women in industry, and in turn, to increase their economic independence. The war and wartime experiences intensified the gradual way in which industrialization was changing the social structure.

Today we find that the role of the American male and female has changed quite drastically. This also revolves around the concept of the double standard. This is the idea that men and women are judged by different sets of standards.

In earlier times the double standard was fixed firmly in place. The man was allowed sexual experiences without injury to his social position or soul. But a woman who went outside of marriage or had pre-marital sexual relations was considered ruined and society considered her to be an outcast.

The modern woman, unlike the woman of old, advertises her sex through the use of clothes, the cosmetics. At social gatherings she is likely to make the first gesture conveying a desire to meet a member of the opposite sex.[3]

These actions are in direct conflict with the beliefs of an earlier time when any exposure was termed bad.

Along with the change in the role of the American female, there has been a change in the role of the American male. He is no longer the element for the survival of the self-sufficient female. The male no longer dominates the American female.

"Women take jobs, earn money, and especially in Washington, put hand to the tiller of the state itself. Men, in the meantime, are encouraged to perform woodworking in the basement, thus becoming homemakers from the ground up, to char steaks in the backyard, thus becoming cooks, and to be active in the Boy Scouts, thus becoming rearers of the young." [4]

The population explosion is a problem in many areas of

---

[3] Tristram Coffin, *The Sex Kick* (New York: MacMillan Company, 1966).
[4] Tristram Coffin, *The Sex Kick* (New York: MacMillan Company, 1966).

the world and this one factor with all its ramifications has been a vital force in reconditioning the thinking about sex.

Facing the problems of over-population, the Americans have been pushed into adopting an intensive but controversial program of birth control. As a result, the Americans no longer view the sex act as a procreative process. Rather, they consider sexual intercourse as an expression of feeling between two individuals. Attitudes regarding abortion are facing liberalization and change. In some countries laws permitting abortion in unwanted pregnancies have been in effect for some time. Just recently have some of the American states passed laws permitting abortion in certain instances. Such occurrences force the public and members of society to view sex and its functions in a different perspective than did their forefathers.

Many observers of the current scene consider the "pill" the most significant single force for increased sexual freedom. The pill makes birth control easier to manage (except for the money requirement), but romantic love is still important; it makes taking the pill, when no definite partner is available, undesirable. What the pill does is to give sexual freedom to those who are having steady sexual relationships, for them the use of the pill adds to romantic love by making elaborate preparations unnecessary.[5]

Still another factor to consider is the evident change in the sexual mores through the exploitation of sex through communication media. We cannot pick up a newspaper, turn on a radio, TV, or go to the movies in America without becoming aware that sex sells everything from cosmetics to automobiles. At one time, an advertiser would indicate to male readers that, if he used a certain product, a pretty girl would kiss him. Now the ads suggest that she will have intercourse with him: "When an Avis girl winks at you she means business," and as Chateau Martin asks, leering only slightly, "Had any lately?" he means have YOU had any lately? Movies have become less suggestive and more obvious; nudity as well as intercourse have become

---

[5] Seiden and Smigel, *The Decline and Fall of the Double Standard* (New York: 1968), quoted in *The Annals of the American Academy of Political & Social Sciences*, Sept. 1968, p. 17.

not uncommon sights. The Scandinavian picture *I, A Woman,* for example, consists of a number of different seductions with a number of different men. Perhaps what is more significant is that censorship boards, the courts, and power groups in this country have sharply amended their definitions of obscenity. The theater has, for some time, been more open about sex and its various ramifications, and four-letter words are becoming a theatrical cliché.[6]

The following quote emphasizes this point.

> In Circleville, Ohio, last fall, the leading theater's lobby was advertising three coming attractions: *Desire in the Dust* (torrid love, infidelity, physical and mental cruelty), *Girl of the Night* (prostitution), and *Dark at the Top of the Stairs* (frigidity).[7]

The effects of this sex exploitation penetrate everywhere and are felt by all, the whole of society. The values are distorted and many of the old ideas become challenged. Youth are caught in a "double-bind." They learn to accept nudity as an ingredient of advertising—then parents and other adults stress different attitudes. Youth cannot understand this sex-saturated society. They feel that by accepting sex matter-of-factly, they may be missing some secret implication, and their confusion is thus compounded.[8]

Dating behavior of teenagers reflects the crossing over of sex roles which pervades so much of the preadolescent years. The teenage girl increasingly is looking for her own satisfaction and may want to be even more equal than her date. Such tendencies have become more important since the 1950's which experienced the first movie about a sexually aggressive teenager (*Susan Slept Here,* 1954), an extraordinarily successful

---

[6] Seiden and Smigel, *The Decline and Fall of the Double Standard* (New York: 1968), quoted in *The Annals of the American Academy of Political & Social Sciences,* Sept. 1968, p. 16.

[7] Don Wharton, "How to Stop the Movies' Sickening Exploitation of Sex," *Readers Digest,* LXXVIII (March, 1961), pp. 37-40.

[8] L. A. Kirkendall and D. C. Calderwood, "Changing Sex Mores and Moral Instruction," *Phi Delta Kappan,* XLIV (October, 1964), pp. 63-68.

novel about a sexually sophisticated girl (*Lolita,* 1958) , and perhaps most important, a series of very popular mannequin dolls, beginning with Betsy McCall in 1954 and culminating in Barbie in 1959. Barbie is a sexy teenager, and playing with her involves changing costumes and thereby preparing for dates.[9]

There exists also in this country a multichotomy of philosophies each uniquely having a modified view of sex. The youth see everything from strict forms of Christianity to total Existentialism and the "free love of the Hippies." The mores of Christianity are presented on the bases of laws and rules while the mores of existentialism are presented with logic. Whether existential philosophy is practical for the individual or not, it is usually preferred because of modern "revolts" against conformity and group behavior.

When buying powder that packs an impressive wallop, the teenager is the pet of the manufacturers, who woo her with sex and encourage her to spend $25 million a year on deodorants, $20 million on lipstick, $9 million on home permanents and millions more on other "essentials." In her 30AA bra and Jackie Kennedy hairdo, she is a living-breathing "femme fatale" at fourteen. There is no time to be a child. "In the first decade of life, the boy and girl learn that love is good and sex is evil; in the second decade, that love is still better, while sex has been upgraded to the status of a forbidden fruit; and in the third decade, that love is better than ever, while sex has suddenly become normal and healthful and is, in fact, a major means of expressing one's higher sentiments." [10]

Advances in science, technology, and disease prevention have lessened the fears of pregnancy and removed the dangers connected with premarital sexual relations. The American society no longer uses the fear of pregnancy and venereal disease as a deterrent to sexual promiscuity. In addition, social dis-

---

[9] Charles Winick, *The Beige Epoch*: *Depolarization of Sex Roles in America* (New York: 1968, quoted in *The Annals of the American Academy of Political and Social Science,* ed. by Thorsten Sellin (Philadelphia, 1968), p. 18.

[10] Richard Hettlinger, *Living With Sex: Student's Dilemma* (New York: The Seabury Press, 1966), p. 4.

approval is not so feared as before, particularly among the adolescent and college set.

The college administrators dryly refer to it as "student cohabitation." To the students themselves, it's better known as "shacking up," "the arrangement," or "living together." Whatever the name, the game is the same and it has become a familiar one at most universities.

It reflects what's happening in America today—the breakdown of Victorian and Protestant ethics; the creation of a whole new set of values, and a new emphasis on honesty and integrity in inter-personal relationships.[11]

To that list, couples quickly add birth control pills, alienation from parents, new liberal student housing rules, drugs, the love philosophy of the hippies, and liberal-minded landlords.

"A couple interviewed by newspaper columnist Judy Klemsrud had this to say: Peter and Susan, age 20, and college sophomores said they had been living together two years, with no wedding plans because they regarded marriage as 'too serious a step.' "[12]

They were honest about everything. They had a joint bank account, and split household experiences, expenses, and chores.

Both students said their grades had improved since they started living together and that the chief advantage of living together was the "emotional security" it offered.

This was only one of several examples I found in my investigation of common living arrangements of college students.

For the unmarried, there is an increasing tendency to reject marriage as the arbitrary dividing line between "socially approved and socially disapproved sexual intimacy." And in the same way that male and female roles have become more equal in other areas of life, greater equality has come to the area of sexual relations: "fair play has been replacing chastity as

---

[11] Judy Klemesrud, "An Arrangement: Living Together for Convenience, Security, Sex," *The New York Times*, March 4, 1968, p. 19.
[12] *Ibid.*, p. 19.

the badge of honor in the interpersonal relations of the sexes." [13]

Sex with "affection" has increasing influence everywhere and finds modes, and discreet supporters in what has always been regarded as strictly "double standard" territory.

To most girls sex is "whatever we can get away with and still be classified nice girls."

Sex in the past decade has become more explicit, rawer, as well as more public. "We gulp our sex straight." Language that would once have prompted a lady to burst into tears or leave the room now punctuates cocktail party chatter.[14]

Another indicator of this generation's expressed attitudes towards sex are the omnipresent buttons, which express not only political, but also sexual opinions. The buttons are designed for fun and shock, and for public declaration for sexual freedom. Sold in large cities all over this country, they range from simple position-statements such as "Make Love, Not War," "I'm for Sexual Freedom," or "Equality for Homosexuals," to invitations which read "Roommate Wanted Apply Within," "Join the Sexual Revolution—Come Home with Me Tonight," to such shock jokes as "Phallic Symbols Arise," "Stand Up for Sex," and "To Come Together is Divine." [15]

All of these factors seem to be related to the change in sexual practices and to the apparent liberalization of sexual standards reflected in the American society today. In this complex and competitive world, sexual needs and satisfactions are inextricably complicated by economic, moral, religious, and social factors which are beyond control and which are entirely ignored. This I have tried to point out by means of using examples of behavior within the United States today. Sex itself is not a problem but one of the fundamental facts of human ex-

---

[13] Seiden and Smigel, *The Decline and Fall of the Double Standard* (New York: 1968), quoted in *The Annals of the American Academy of Political & Social Sciences*, Sept. 1968, p. 14.

[14] Gael Green, *Sex and the College Girl* (New York: Dell Publishing Co., 1964), p. 61.

[15] Seiden and Smigel, *The Decline and Fall of the Double Standard* (New York: 1968), quoted in *The Annals of the American Academy of Political & Social Sciences*, Sept. 1968, p. 16.

istence; yet adolescents grow up in a society which treats it as a problem.

Youngsters today grow up in a context of a sort of public schizophrenia, in a society which is "sex-centric, but sex rejecting." Parents encourage, or at least endorse a system of dating, which from, the age of prepuberty, utilizes all the traditional forms of elementary endearment and initial love-making in the game of casual relationships. Adolescents are pushed into adult situations far too early, often by mothers, who want them to be well-adjusted and who see in their children's popularity and "maturity" a substitute for the success they themselves failed to achieve. Parents cannot be all to blame, as the adult society as a whole (of which parents form a good percentage) uses every possible form of visual sexual titillation to market its wares, and commercial interests thrive on worthless pornographic literature and crude "skin flicks." TV shows and movies take it for granted that the only possible reason for a man and a woman being together is to hop into bed; but when teenagers do what they have obviously been invited to do, society either punishes them or looks embarrassingly the other way. A quick glance at the magazine racks or the paperback stand in almost any drug store will confirm that sex is one of the most lucrative commodities on the market today. Padded brassieres are available to twelve-year-old girls. Despite the tremendous increase in the public representation of sex and the break-up of 19th-century standards of censorship, the 20th-century has done perhaps a worse job than any other in helping its youth to come to terms with this profoundly difficult subject.[16]

The consequences of this breakdown of communication between adults and adolescents may be far more serious than we sometimes realize. The fact that information about sex is, sooner or later, picked up from the peer group does not mean that the emotional attitude toward this knowledge is what it

---

[16] Hettlinger, *Living With Sex: Student's Dilemma* (New York: The Seabury Press, 1966), pp. 1-3.

would have been if the parental role had been adequately played.[17]

Another point to consider is the attitude of scientific inquiry into all beliefs and practices of man. This also includes his sex life. Alfred Kinsey, Masters and Johnson, and others, have used the scientific approach to sex and man's sexual behavior. Volunteers are used to study male and female reactions in the sexual act—admittedly to gain a completely objective approach to the whole phenomenon of sex.[18]

The changes in the sexual mores which have occurred in recent times have implications for all who are involved in providing sex education. Those who are usually involved in this procedure have a definite interest in youth. A good sex education program is a joint effort on the part of parents, schools, churches, and the community as a whole.

Attitudes about sex should also be taught in high school. The college freshman is thrown into the multichotomy of philosophies on sex and there is quite an emotional conflict in the rapid changes of personal sex views. He wishes to be socially accepted and will conform to what he "thinks" is an acceptable norm.

Parents have the basic responsibility for sex education from the standpoint of emotional tone and spirituality. Basic values are instilled in the family relationship. Attitudes toward sex are usually acquired in the home. Often, parents avoid discussions with their children because of a lack of knowledge or a feeling of inadequacy in the areas of sex. This lack of knowledge or inadequacy could possibly be changed in some form of sex education for the adult population. Also, a better understanding of present-day attitudes toward sex-related problems might influence parents to become better listeners when their children ask questions or express opinions.[19]

The church along with the home plays a role in regard to

---

[17] Greg Foster, "Sex Information vs. Sex Education," *Implications for School Health*, XXXVII (May, 1967), pp. 248-50.

[18] Coffin, *The Sex Kick* (New York: MacMillan Company, 1966).

[19] Dean Knudson and Hallowell Pope, "Premarital Sex Norms, the Family and Social Change," *Journal of Marriage and the Family*, XXVII (August, 1965), pp. 314-17.

instilling attitudes and values. Conventional sexual standards have been based on negative deterrents such as fear of pregnancy and venereal disease. With medical advancements in birth control techniques and antibiotics, these possible outcomes of premarital sex no longer hold the fear-producing inhibitions they once did. The greatest change is the idea that ethics and morality are no longer taught as absolute values. A new ethics called "situational ethics" considers the person involved and the circumstances, before condoning or condemning sexual relations outside the marriage relationship.

The implications for the schools are more easily defined. Due to the technological approach to problems today, youth wants as complete an answer as possible to a question. They also demand truthful and sincere answers.

The schools need well-trained teachers in the area of sex education. These are teachers who can develop the type of rapport with students which will provide the atmosphere conducive to good discussions—an atmosphere which lets students feel free to ask questions and express opinions. This type of teacher should be emotionally mature and one who also has knowledge about the subject and how to teach it. Teacher preparation improvements is one way to alleviate the problems of sex education in the schools.

The community at large should be made aware of the need for sex education in the schools and to encourage such programs in their development. Approaches to adult education might be made through parent-teacher groups, public health agencies or adult education courses provided by the public school system. Most authorities in the field of sex education agree that community support is essential for the success of any sex education program.

# CHAPTER XI

# People in the United States and How They Use Their Leisure Time

Nearly two thousand years ago Aristotle wrote that "if every tool when summoned, or even of its own accord, could do the work that befits it, then there would be no need of either workers by masters or of slaves by lords."[1] Automation and modern industrial methods alone cannot produce the social and economic structure that Aristotle envisioned, but they have already had far-reaching effects. Among these is the gradual but steady decline in working hours which is changing our attitudes toward both work and play. In recent years the ways in which we use our leisure time have been the subject of comment and discussion by social critics expressing many points of view. Much as the critics differ, they all seem to confirm Bertrand Russel's observation that "to be able to fill leisure intelligently is the last product of civilization."[2]

A hundred years ago, the average workweek in the United States was about seventy hours. Today, it is about forty hours; and experts say that in the next decade or so it will be cut again, the predictions ranging from thirty-seven hours or thereabouts down to twenty or even less. This reduction might come as a shorter workday, or fewer workdays per week or longer—very much longer—vacations.

---

[1] Pauline Madow, *Recreation in America* (New York: The H. W. Wilson Company, 1965), p. 1.
[2] *Ibid.*, p. 1.

In the last few decades, leisure has brought about a profound alteration in the patterns of our society. A hundred years ago, nearly everybody worked very long hours, six or seven days a week, and family vacations were almost unknown. Rich men might send their wives and children to the seashore or the mountains in the summer, but rarely joined them for more than a few hours a week at most. Poor people, the overwhelming majority, had no vacations; their free time consisted of holidays of one or two day's duration.

Men and boys went hunting and fishing, but this was more to get food than as recreation. On special occasions like the Fourth of July, there were athletic events or chasing a young, greased pig, but many watched and few participated.

The products of American industry have also influenced leisure time. Household appliances have relieved women of much tedious housework. Frozen, canned, and concentrated foods have made it easier to prepare means, and the automobile has made it very easy to get from place to place, and thus saving more and more time. Such advances help explain how so many American homemakers find time for so many types of activities.

Improved medical care has given Americans longer life expectancy through the years. Since 1900 the average length of life has increased from 47 years to more than 68 years. This also has increased the percentage of older people in the population. In 1879 only 3 of every 100 were 65 or older; in 1950 the number had increased to 7 of every 100. The prediction for 1975 is that more than 9 of every 100 will be 65 or older.[3] So now, more than ever, there are more people who have spare time to utilize.

The productivity of America's free enterprise system has earned the people more and more leisure time. The problem now arises as to how the American people spend these leisure hours.

Today they are seeing an astonishing "recreation explo-

---

[3] Lloyd W. Warner, *American Life* (Chicago: The University of Chicago Press, 1953).

sion." [4] They spend from $30 billion to $40 billion annually, perhaps as much as twenty times more per capita than they did in 1900. Max Kaplan, in his book *Leisure in America* reports that in 1959, 33 million people went swimming at least once, fishing was enjoyed by 32 million, dancing by 32 million, bowling by 18 million, hunting by 16 million. Baseball, professional and amateur, regular or softball, is played by 18 million, golf by 8 million and tennis by 4 million.

To help Americans use their spare time, cities and towns maintain playgrounds, golf courses, parks, and swimming pools. The Federal and state governments operate large parks and other recreation areas.

Other forms of outdoor recreation have also mushroomed. Skiing had not reached the United States in 1900, and water skiing and scuba diving had not been invented, but now millions participate in these sports. They spent more than $100 annually on fishing and hunting licenses, and $1 billion on gardening equipment, seeds, and plants.

President Lyndon B. Johnson pledged his administration to certain conservation and recreational policies in his State of the Union Message of 1965. "We must have a massive effort to save the countryside and establish a green legacy for tomorrow, more large and small parks, more seashores and open spaces than have been created during any period in our history." He spoke also of his intention to "landscape highways and provide places of relaxation and recreation wherever our roads run." [5] The Federal Government has already undertaken to finance in large part a 4,100 mile highway system over which recreational travel is expected to exceed 50 billion miles each year. Later, on February 8, 1965, the President detailed his program for outdoor recreation in a special message to Congress on natural beauty.

In addition, the federal government has played a major role in opening recreational facilities to all of its citizens. On

---

[4] Madow, *Recreation in America* (New York: The H. W. Wilson Company 1965), p. 11.

[5] Madow, *Recreation in America* (New York: The H. W. Wilson Company, 1965), p. 54.

October 20, 1958, the Supreme Court emphasized its position against racial discrimination in tax-supported facilities such as municipal parks, playgrounds, and golf courses. In 1964 Congress approved the Civil Rights Law, which prohibits racial discrimination in public accommodations, such as restaurants, motels, and places of amusement that are involved in interstate commerce. This prohibition was unanimously upheld by the Supreme Court on December 14, 1964.

Besides recreation in the out-of-doors, the Federal Government is concerned with other leisure-time activities. For example, Congress enacted the Library Services Act of 1956 providing motives for expansion of library facilities over a five-year period and in 1961 extended the law for another five years. In a related area Congress approved the Adult Education Act of 1962, authorizing funds for instruction of adults deficient in reading and writing skills. The government takes an interest, too, in what is perhaps the most popular form of indoor relaxation, watching television. Its Federal Communication Commission has regulatory authority under the standard of public interest, convenience, and necessity over radio and television transmission.

Another aspect of government operations affecting leisure time is the Social Security System. The system handles over $12 billion annually for benefits to older people, many experiencing enforced full-time leisure.

Americans spend much of their leisure time at home. While hardly a sport, television is of course the most popular of all types of passive recreation. Television has reinforced the disease of "spectatoritis." In less than two decades, it has grown to the point where people spend seven-eighths as much time watching it as they spend at work! In 1964, Americans occupied nearly 300 billion person-hours in front of the screen—or at least, with their sets turned on. Television brings entertainment into the living-room, and high-fidelity stereophonic phonographs make the home a concert hall. Book and magazine reading also play a large part in home leisure-time activities. They buy more than a quarter of a billion paperbacks each year.

Spectator sports have expanded similarly—far beyond the increase in population. Kaplan says that 28 million watch baseball annually; 23 million, football; 18 million, basketball; and 9 million, horse racing.

Not only has recreation expanded enormously, but it has been upgraded culturally. In 1900 there were 100 symphony orchestras in the country; today there are about 1200. America now has more than 1500 local theater groups, most of them amateurs. People spend $500 million annually on concert tickets. In 1934, 500 records of Beethoven's Ninth Symphony were bought, as in 1954, 75,000. Twenty million Americans play the piano, 4 million the violin. There are 2 million "Sunday painters." [6]

Sixty years ago, very few employers paid any attention to what their workers did in their spare time, though some did arrange an annual "company picnic." Today the picture is wholly changed. Many big firms maintain vacation retreats and often they provide playing fields for their employees.

Most Americans regard an annual vacation as a natural and essential element in their lives. During the 1920's employers began to accept the idea of giving employees two weeks vacations with pay. Others increased this to three weeks and sometimes even more. Each summer, millions of Americans pack their suitcases and head for their favorite recreation areas. They travel in comfortable automobiles over paved highways to state and national parks, to summer resorts, or to the great cities. Air travel has made it easier for many to vacation in Europe or other foreign lands. Great resort areas in Hawaii, Florida, Arizona, and elsewhere attract persons seeking a few days or a few weeks of sunshine in midwinter. The tourist industry plays an important, thriving part in the nation's economic life.

One of the results of the new leisure is the do-in-yourselfer.[7] He uses part of his spare time to make repairs, to build furniture, or perhaps even to remodel his home. Entertaining friends

---

[6] Madow, *Recreation in America* (New York: The H. W. Wilson Company, 1965), p. 11.

[7] "United States," *The World Book Encyclopedia*, 1961, Vol. XVIII.

at home has become more than ever a part of the American life.

Every year, thousands of Americans enroll in various kinds of study courses to broaden their education and experiences. Others learn music, photography, or painting. Millions spend much of their leisure time taking part in local government and community-service groups.

While camping is not a new activity, it is undergoing a re-emphasis as an education medium. The popularity of school camps, community camps, and day camps, is virtually taking the country by storm. This is justly so since camping offers a most interesting and natural setting for the learning process. Moreover, crowded city living, with its emphasis on brick, cement, and steel, has made little provision for nature. Even for the lad who comes from a country setting, the camp offers a desirable setting for learning to get along with others, practicing the give and take communal living, and developing self-reliance in the out-of-doors.

Let us think of the American attitude toward time. There is here a certain horror of any span of time which a man might have at his own disposal in order to do nothing. The great value and efficacy of standing idle, and lingering over one's dream, is little appreciated in this country. One might wonder, for instance, whether committee meetings and all similar periodically recurrent administrative nuisances have not been invented to prevent professors, once they have finished lecturing, from having any time for idleness—that is to say, for thinking at leisure and pursuing their own research.

Well, friendship requires a great waste of time, and much idleness; creative things require a great deal of idleness. So it is that leisure constitutes a serious problem for American life; especially given the social and technical progress, the automation, for instance, which makes working hours shorter and shorter in industry.

The question will be to have leisure time occupied in a manner really profitable to man, and not entirely taken up by the sort of stupefying passivity that is more often than not developed by movies or television.

Real recreation is something which not only gives pleasure, but also helps to renew, or recreate, the mind and the body. Therefore, the kind of recreation we engage in is important to all of us. If man spends his time wisely, he can greatly enrich his life. His recreation can help him to recover new talents, and to improve himself both physically and mentally. Society in general reaches a higher level of culture when large numbers of persons have time to develop their personalities and interests to the fullest possible extent. For this reason, recreation is of social as well as individual importance. It is becoming more and more important to realize that leisure time should be spent wisely and profitably; for in this world, we are being faced with this problem of too much leisure time.

# Bibliography

## BOOKS

Ackerman, Nathan W. *The Psychodynamics of Family Life*. New York: Basic Book Inc., 1958.

Adams, Charles, *Common Sense in Advertising*. New York: Mac-Manus, John & Adams, Inc., pp. 105, 119-120.

Alexander, George J. *Honesty and Competition*. Syracuse, New York: Syracuse University Press, 1967.

Allen, Steve. *The Ground Is Our Table*. Garden City, New York: Doubleday and Co., 1966.

Anderson, John E. *The Psychology of Development and Personal Adjustment*. New York: Henry Holt & Co., 1949.

Angell, Robert Cooley, *The Integration of American Society*. New York and London: McGraw-Hill Book Co., Inc., 1941.

Angyal, Andras, M.D., Ph.D. *Foundations for a Science of Personality*. New York: The Commonwealth Fund, 1941.

Anshen, Ruth Nanda. *The Family: Its Function and Destiny*. New York: Harper & Brothers, 1959.

Arons, Leon, and May, Mark A., ed. *Television and Human Behavior*. New York: Appleton-Century Crofts, 1963.

Aurback, Herbert A. *The Status of Housing of Negroes in Pittsburgh*. Mayor's Commission on Human Relations, 1958.

Ayers, C. E. *Towards Reasonable Society*. Austin: University of Texas Press, 1961.

Bagehot, Walter. *The English Constitution*. London, New York and Toronto: Oxford University Press, 1928.

Barnes, Harry Elmer and Ruedi, Oreen M. and Ferguson, Robert H. *The American Way of Life*. New York: Prentice-Hall, Inc., 1942.

Bates, Charles A. *Good Advertising*. New York: Holmes Publishing Co., 1896.

Bedell, Clyde. *How to Write Advertising that Sells*. New York: McGraw-Hill Book Co., Inc., 1952, 273.

Benjamin, Harold, ed. *Education for Social Control*. Philadelphia, 1935.

Bensman, Joseph. *Dollars and Sense*. New York: The MacMillan Co., 1967.

Benson, Purnell Handy. *Religion in Contemporary Culture*. New York: Harper and Brothers, 1960.

Berelson, Bernard and Janowitz. *Public Opinion and Communication*. Glencoe, Illinois: The Free Press, 1950.

Bernard, Jessie. *American Family Behavior*. Harper & Brothers, 1942.

Berry, Brewton. *Race and Ethnic Relations*. Boston: Houghton Mifflin Co., 1965.

Bertrand, Alvin L. *An Introduction to Theory and Method, Basic Sociology*, New York: Appleton-Century Crofts, 1967.

Blitsten, Dorothy R. *The World of the Family*. New York: Random House, 1963.

Boas, Franz. *Race and Democratic Society*. New York: J. J. Augustin Publisher, 1945.

Bogardus, Emery S. *Sociology*. 4th ed. New York: MacMillan Co., 1954.

Bogart, Leo. *Psychology In Media Strategy*. Chicago: American Marketing Association, 1966.

Bontemps, Arna. *Story of the Negro*. New York: Alfred A. Knopf,

Borden, Neil H. *Advertising in Our Economy*. Chicago: Richard D. Irwin, Inc., 1945.

Bott, Elizabeth. *Family and Social Networks*. London: Tavistock Publications Limited, 1965.

Bredermeier, Harry C., and Toby, Jackson. *Social Problems in America*. New York: John Wiley & Sons, Inc., 1966.

Brembeck, Cole S. *Social Foundations of Education*. New York: John Wiley and Sons, Inc., 1966.

Brewster, Arthur J. *Introduction to Advertising*. New York: McGraw-Hill Book Co., Inc., 1947.

Brim, Orville G., Jr. *Socialization After Childhood—Two Essays*. New York: John Wiley & Son, Inc., 1966.

Brown, Francis. *One America*. New York: Prentice-Hall, 1955.

Brown, J. F. *Psychology and the Social Order*. New York: McGraw-Hill Book Co., Inc., 1936.

Burns, James MacGregor, and Peltason, Jack Walter. *Government by the People*. Englewood Cliffs, N. J.: Prentice-Hall, Inc., 1960.

Burton, Philip Ward. *Principles of Advertising*. Englewood Cliffs, New Jersey: Prentice-Hall, Inc., 1955.

Burtt, Harold E. *Psychology of Advertising*. Boston: Houghton Mifflin Co., 1938.

Caples, John. *Making Ads Pay*. New York: Harper & Brothers Publishers, 1957.

Caples, John. *Tested Advertising Methods*. New York: Harper & Brothers, 1961.

Carrier, Herve. *The Society of Religious Belonging*. New York: Herder and Herder, 1965.

Carson, Clarence. *The American Tradition*. New York: The Foundation for Economic Education, Inc., 1964.

Christenson, Reo M., and McWilliams, Robert O. *Voice of the People*. St. Louis: McGraw Hill Book Co., 1967.

Coffin, Tristram. *The Sex Kick*. New York: MacMillan Company, 1966.

Cole, G. D. H. *Studies in Class Structure*. London: Rutledge and Kegan Paul, 1955.

Coleman, James C. *Abnormal Psychology & Modern Life*. Chicago: Scott, Foresman & Co., 1958.

Collier, John. *The Indians of the Americas*. New York: W. W. Norton & Co., Inc., 1947.

Crawford, John W. *Advertising*. Boston: Allyn and Bacon, Inc., 1965.

Dahlke, H. Otto. *Values in Culture and Classroom*. New York: Harper and Brothers, 1958.

Daniels, Walter M., ed. *American Indians*. New York: The H. W. Wilson Co., 1957.

Davis, Allison. *Social-Class Influences Upon Learning*. Cambridge: Harvard University Press, 1955.

Douglas, Mary, Barry, Sir Gerald; Bronowski, Dr. J.; Fisher, James; and Huxley, Sir Julian. *Man in Society*. Garden City: Doubleday Co., Inc., 1964.

Duncan, Otis and Beverly. *The Negro Population of Chicago*. Chicago: University of Chicago Press, 1957.

Dunn, S. Watson. *Advertising—Its Role in Modern Marketing*. New York: Holt, Rinehart, and Winston, 1961.

Elinson, Howard, and Murphy, Raymond J. *Problems and Pros-*

126

*pects of the Negro Movements.* Beltmont, California: Wadsworth Publishing Co., Inc., 1966.

Emery, Edwin; Ault, Philip H.; and Agee, Warren R. *Introduction to Mass Communications.* Dodd, Mead & Co., Inc., 1960.

Epstein, Abraham. *Insecurity a Challenge to America.* New York: Harrison Smith and Robert Hass, 1933.

Fey, Harold E. and McNickle, D'Arcy. *Indians and Other Americans.* New York: Harper & Brothers, 1959.

Field, Marshall. *Freedom Is More Than a Word.* Chicago: University of Chicago Press, 1945.

Frey, Albert Wesley. *Advertising.* New York: The Ronald Press Co., 1953.

Fromm, Erich. *Escape from Freedom.* New York: Rinehart & Co., Inc., 1941.

Fromm, Erich. *Man for Himself.* New York: Rinehart & Co., Inc., 1947.

Fromm, Erich. *The Sane Society.* New York: Rinehart & Co., Inc., 1955.

Fromme, Allan. *Our Troubled Selves.* New York: Farrar, Straus & Giroux, 1967.

Gaw, Walter A. *Advertising: Methods and Media.* San Francisco: Wadsworth Publishing Co., Inc., 1961.

Gist and Fava. *Urban Society.* New York: Thomas Y. Crowell Co., 1964.

Gluckman, Max. *Closed Systems and Open Minds: The Limits of Naivete in Social Anthropology.* Chicago: Aldine Publishing Co., 1964.

Goode, Kenneth M., and Powel, Harford, Jr., *What About Advertising?* New York: Harper & Brothers, 1929.

Gordon, Milton Myron. *Assimilation in American Life.* New York: Oxford University Press, 1964.

Grazia, Sebastian de. *Of Time, Work and Leisure.* New York: The Twentieth Century Fund, 1962.

Green, Gail. *Sex and the College Girl.* New York: Dell Publishing Co., 1964.

Griffin, Alan F. *Freedom American Style.* New York: Henry Holt & Co., 1940.

Groves, Ernest R. *The Family and Its Social Functions.* New York: J. B. Lippincott Co., 1940.

Hall, Edward T. *The Silent Language.* New York: Doubleday and Co., 1959.

Halsey, A. H.; Floud, Jean; and Anderson, D. Arnold. *Education, Economy, and Society.* The Free Press of Glencoe, 1962.

Handlin, Oscar. *The Uprooted.* Boston: Little, Brown and Co., 1951.

Harrington, Michael. *The Other America.*

Havishurst, Robert J., and Neugarten, Bernice L. *Society and Education.* Boston: Allyn and Bacon, Inc., 1967.

Herberg, Will. *Protestant-Catholic-Jew.* New York: Doubleday & Co., 1955.

Herriott, Robert E., and St. John, Nancy Hoyt. *Social Class and the Urban School.* New York: John Wiley & Sons, Inc., 1966.

Herskovits, Melville J. *The American Negro.* New York: Alfred A. Knopf, 1958.

Heschel, Abraham. *The Insecurity of Freedom.* New York: Farrar, Straus & Giroux, 1966.

Hettlinger, Richard, *Living with Sex: Student's Dilemma.* New York: The Seabury Press, 1966.

*History of Thucydides, The.* Trans. by Benjamin Jowett. New York: The Tandy-Thomas Company, 1909.

Hollingshead, A. B. *Elmtown's Youth.* New York: John Wiley and Sons, 1949.

Hook, Bidney. *The Paradoxes of Freedom.* Berkeley: University of California Press, 1962.

Hunt, Elgin F., and Karlin, Jules. *Society Today and Tomorrow.* New York: Macmillan Co., 1967.

Hurlock, Elizabeth B. *Child Development.* New York, San Francisco, Toronto, and London: McGraw-Hill Book Co., Inc., 1959.

Jaspers, Karl. *Man in the Modern Age.* Garden City, New York: Doubleday & Co., Inc., 1933, rev. 1951.

Javits, Jacob K. *Discrimination—U.S.A.* New York: Harcourt, Brace and Co., 1960.

Josephson, Eric & Mary, ed. *Man Alone—Alienation in Modern Society.* New York: Dell Publishing Co., Inc., 1962.

Kellaway, George P. *Education for Living.* Great Britain: Cambridge University Press, 1967.

Kendler, Howard H. *Basic Psychology.* Santa Barbara, California: Appleton-Century-Crofts, 1963.

Kennedy, John F. *A Nation of Immigrants.* New York: Harper and Row, 1964.

128

Klapper, Joseph T. *The Effects of Mass Media*. New York: Bureau of Applied Social Research, Columbia University, 1949.

Knight, Everett. *The Objective Society*. London: Routledge and Kegan Paul, 1959.

Kraus, Edward C. *Origins of Conflict*. New York: Vantage Press, 1964.

Kulp, Danniel H., II. *Educational Sociology*. New York, London, and Toronto: Longmans, Greenand Co., 1932.

Kung, H. W. *Chinese in American Life*. Seattle: University of Washington Press, 1962.

Landi, Paul H. *Social Control*. Chicago: J. B. Lippincott Co., 1939.

Lasher, George Struss, ed. *Baird's Manual of American College Fraternities*. Menaska, Wisconsin: Collegiate Press, George Banta Co., Inc., 1957.

Lazarsfeld, Paul F. *Psychological Impact of Newspaper and Radio Advertisement*. Chicago: 1949.

Lazarsfeld, Paul F. and Berelson. *The Effects of Mass Communication*. Glencoe, Illinois: The Free Press, 1960.

Lazarsfeld, Paul F. *The Responsibilities of American Advertising, 1920-1940*. New Haven: Yale University Press, 1958.

Lenski, Gerhard Emanuel. *Power and Prejudice*. New York: McGraw-Hill, 1966.

Lerner, Max. *America As a Civilization*. New York: Simon & Schuster, 1957.

Leslie, Gerald R. *The Family in Social Context*. New York: Oxford University Press, 1967.

Lindgren, Henry Clay. *Meaning: Antidote to Anxiety*. New York: Thomas Nelson & Sons, 1956.

Lindquest, Calvert. *How to Tell if Your Ads Will Sell*. Chicago: 1950.

*Living Letters*. Wheaton, Illinois: Tyndale House, 1962.

Lyon, Marguerite. *And So to Bedlam*. New York: The Bobbs-Merrill Co., 1943.

MacIver, R. M. *Group Relations and Group Antagonisms*. Binghamton, New York: Vail-Ballou Press, 1944.

MacIver, R. M. *Integrity and Compromise*. New York: The Institute for Religious and Social Studies, Distributor, or Harper & Brothers, 1957.

Mack, Raymond W. *Race, Color, Power*. New York: American Book Co., 1963.

Madow, Pauline. *Recreation in America.* New York: The H. W. Wilson Co., 1965.

McDonagh, Edward C., and Simpson, Jon E., ed. *Social Problems: Persistent Challenges.* New York: Holt, Rinehart & Winston, Inc., 1965.

McWilliams, Carey. *Brothers Under the Skin.* Boston: Little, Brown and Co., 1951.

Meltzer, Milton, and August Meier. *Time of Trial, Time of Hope.* Garden City, New York: Doubleday and Co., 1966.

Merton, Robert K. *Social Theory & Social Structure.* New York: The Free Press of Glencoe, 1957.

Montagu, Ashley. *Education and Human Relations.* New York: Grove Press, Inc., 1958.

Montagu, Ashley. *The Humanization of Man.* Cleveland & New York: The World Publishing Co., 1962.

Morley, John. *On Compromise.* London: MacMillan and Co., 1891.

Mussen, Paul H. *The Psychological Development of the Child.* Englewood Cliffs, New Jersey: 1967.

Myshne, Davis A. Trans. *Public Education in the U.S.S.R.* Moscow: Propem Publishers.

*New English Bible.* London: Cambridge University Press, 1961.

O'Hara, Robert C. *Media for the Millions.* New York: Random House, 1961.

Packard, Vance Oakly. *The Status Seekers.* New York: D. McKay Co., 1959.

Packard, Vance Oakly. *The Hidden Persuaders.* New York: D. McKay Co., 1957.

Pappenheim, Fritz. *The Alienation of Modern Man.* New York: Monthly Review Press, 1959.

Parsons, Talcott. *Essays in Sociological Theory.* New York: The Free Press of Glencoe. 1954.

Peterson, Theodore; Jensen, Jay W.; and Rivers,, William L. *The Mass Media and Modern Society.* Chicago: Holt, Rinehart, and Winston, Inc., 1965.

Phillips, Derek L. *Studies in American Society: II.* New York: Thomas Y. Crowell Co., 1967.

Pounds, Ralph L., and Bryner, James. *The School in American Society.* 2nd ed. New York: The Macmillan Co., 1967.

Quinn, James, and Repke, Arthur. *Living in a Social World.* Chicago: J. B. Lippincott Co., 1956.

Rodehaver, Myles W.; Axtell, William B.; and Gross, Richard E.

*The Sociology of the School.* New York: Thomas Y. Crowell Co., 1957.

Rose, Arnold. *The Negro in America.* Boston: The Beacon Press, 1959.

Rose, Arnold and Caroline. *America Divided.* New York: A. A. Knopf, 1960.

Rowan, Carl T., and Spangler, Earl. *The Negro in Minnesota.* Minneapolis, Minnesota: T. S. Dennison and Co., Inc., 1961.

Rudy, Willis. *Schools in an Age of Mass Culture.* New Jersey: Prentice-Hall, Inc., 1965.

Sargent, Stansfield, and Williamson, Robert C. *Social Psychology.* New York: Ronald Press, 1966.

Schramm, Wilbur. *Mass Media and National Development.* Stanford, California: Stanford University Press, 1964.

Schramm, Wilbur. *Responsibility in Mass Communication.* New York: Harper & Brothers, 1957.

Schwab, Victor. *How to Write a Good Advertisement.* New York: Harper & Row.

Scott, Walter Dill. *The Psychology of Advertising in Theory and Practice.* Boston: Small, Maynard and Co., 1921.

Scott, William A. *Values and Organizations.* Chicago: Rand McNally Co., 1965.

Shaftel, Frannie R., and Shaftel, George. *Role Playing for Social Values, and Decision Making in the Social Studies.* Englewood Cliffs, New Jersey: Prentice-Hall, Inc.

Shaw, Franklin J., and Ort, Robert S. *Personal Adjustment in American Culture.* New York: Harper and Brothers, 1953.

Sheen, Fulton J. *Peace of Soul.* New York: McGraw-Hill Book Co., 1949.

Simpson, George Eaton, and Yinger, J. Milton. *Racial and Cultural Minorities (An Analysis of Prejudices and Discrimination).* New York: Harper and Brother, 1953.

Smigel, Erwin, and Seiden, Rita. *The Decline and Fall of the Double Standard.* New York: 1968. Quoted in *The Annals of the American Academy of Political & Social Sciences.* Sept. 1968.

Soreson, Herbert, and Malm, Marguerite. *Psychology for Living.* New York: McGraw-Hill Book Co., Inc., 1957.

Spangler, Earl. *The Negro in America.* Minneapolis: Lerner Publication Co., 1966.

Spindler, George D. *Education and Culture.* Chicago: Holt, Rinehart, and Winston, Inc., 1963.

Spurrier, Richard B. *The Overpopulated Society*. New York: Exposition Press, 1967.

Stein, Maurice R.; Vidich, Arthur J.; and White, David M., ed. *Identity & Anxiety*. Illinois: The Free Press of Glencoe, 1960.

Steinberg, Charles S. *Mass Media Communication*. New York: Hastings House, 1966.

Steiner, Heiri, and Gebser, Jean. *Anxiety—A Condition of Modern Man*. New York: Dell Publishing Co., 1962.

Taplin, Walter. *Advertising*: *A New Approach*. Boston: Little, Brown and Co., 1960.

Thayer, V. T., and Levit, Martin. *The Role of the School in American Society*. New York: Dodd, Mead and Co., 1966.

Turner, Ralph H., and Killian, Lewis M. *Collective Behavior*. Englewood Cliffs, New Jersey: Prentice-Hall, Inc., 1957.

Tyler, Poyntz. *Advertising in America*. New York: The W. W. Wilson Co., 1959.

U.S. Bureau of the Census. *Statistical Abstracts of the United States*. 1959, pp. 219-318.

Vincent, William S. *Roles of the Citizen—Principles and Practices*. Evanston, Illinois: Row, Peterson & Co., 1959.

Walbach, T. Walter, *et al. Civilization Past and Present*. Chicago: Scott, Foresman, 1965.

Warner, William Lloyd. *American Life*. Chicago: The University of Chicago Press, 1953.

Warner, William L. *Status System of Modern Community*. New York: Yale University Press, 1942.

Warner, William L., and Lent, Paul S. *The Social Life of a Modern Community*. New Haven: Yale University Press, 1941

Westby-Gibson, Dorothy. *Social Perspective on Education*. New York: John Wiley & Sons, Inc., 1965.

Wheelis, Allen. *The Quest for Identity*. New York: W. W. Norton & Co., Inc., 1958.

Winick, Charles. *The Beige Epoch*: *Depolarization of Sex Roles in America*. New York: 1968. Quoted in *The Annals of the American Academy of Political and Social Science*, ed. by Thorsten Sellin. Philadelphia, 1968.

Winter, Gibson. *The Suburban Captivity of the Churches*. Garden City, New York: Doubleday, 1961.

Wood, Robert C. *Suburbia—Its People and Their Politics*. Boston: Houghton Mifflin Co.

Woodson, Carter G., and Wesley, Charles H. *The Negro in Our*

*Society*. Washington, D. C.: The Associated Publishers, Inc., 1966.

Woodward, C. Van. *The Strange Career of Jim Crow*. New York: Oxford University Press, 1966.

Wright, John S., and Warner, Daniel S. *Advertising*. New York: McGraw-Hill Book Co., Inc., 1962.

Wynn, John Charles. *Sex, Family and Society in Theological Focus*. New York: Association Press, 1966.

Zacher, Robert V. *Advertising Techniques and Management*. Homewood, Illinois: Richard D. Irwin, 1967.

## PERIODICALS

"After the Riots: A Survey," *Newsweek*, August 21, 1967.

Biddle, Francis, "Necessity of Compromise," *Integrity and Compromise*, ed. by R. M. MacIvers. New York: Harper & Brothers, 1957.

Brucker, Herbert, "Mass Man and Mass Media," *Saturday Review*. XLVIII. May 29, 1965.

Chein, Isador, "Some Considerations in Intergroup Prejudice" *Journal of Educational Psychology*.

Dillingham, Harry G., "Protestant Religion and Social Status," *American Journal of Sociology*. LXX, Jan. 1965.

Foster, Greg, "Sex Information vs. Sex Education," *Implications for School Health*, XXXVII, May, 1967.

Jones, Douglas R., "Pressure on Adolescents," *Education Leader*, December, 1965.

Kael, Pauline, "Spoofing & Schtik," *The Atlantic*, 84:5.

Kaselow, Joseph, "How's That Again," *Saturday Review*, 48:56, July, 1965.

Kirkendall, L. A. and Calderwood, D. "Changing Sex Mores and Moral Instruction," *Phi Delta Kappa*, XLIV, 1964.

Lazarus, George, "The Knock in Advertising," *Saturday Review*, December, 1965.

Loveman, Amy, "Weapons of Will," *Saturday Review*, XXXV, November, 1952.

Lowe, William, "The Decision to Differ," *House and Garden*, CXI, April, 1957.

McCarthy, Brian, "Age of Conformity," *Commonweal*, LXVI, June 19, 1957.

Maslow, Mill and Robinson, Joseph B., "Civil Rights Legislation and the Fight for Equality, 1862-1952," *The University of Chicago Law Review.*

Meier, Arnold, *et al.,* "Detroit Citizenship Education Study," *A Curriculum for Citizenship,* 1952.

Mitchum, John C. and Anna Maria, "Minority Child," *The Instructor,* April, 1968.

Ogburn, William F., "The Changing Family," *The Family,* 1938.

Pope, Hallowell and Knudson, Dean, "Premarital Sex Norms, the Family and Social Change," *Journal of Marriage and the Family,* XXVII, August, 1965.

"Rise of the Negro."

Roper, Elmo, "Advertising in the 1970's," *Saturday Review,* Feb., 1965.

Shayon, Robert L., "The Art of Bamboozlement," *Saturday Review,* July, 1965.

Taylor, Harold, "The Closed and the Open Society," *Challenges of the Sixties,* Washington, D. C., Dept. of Agriculture, 1963.

Vivante, "The Talk of the Town," *The New Yorker,* 1965.

"Welcome to U.S.A. Citizenship," United States Department of Justice, M-76.

Wharton, Don, "How to Stop the Movies' Sickening Exploitation of Sex," *Readers Digest,* LXXVIII, March, 1961.

Winebrenner, D. K., "Keeping in Line," *School Arts,* LIX, December, 1959.

Zeller, Charles N., "Indian Education: Another National Problem," *Scholastic Teacher,* March, 1968.

## NEWSPAPER ARTICLES

Klemesrud, Judy, "An Arrangement: Living Together for Convenience, Security, Sex," *The New York Times,* March 4, 1968.

Ribuffoni, Dean, "Freedom of the Press: A Relative Thing," and "The Right to Know," *Egyptian,* S.I.U., Carbondale, Illinois, vol. 44, April 20, 1968.

"Reporters Stage Fake Crimes, Prove Apathy is Great," *St. Louis Post-Dispatch,* Nov. 26, 1967.

## UNPUBLISHED MATERIALS

Counts, George S., Professor, adaption from speech.